IN HER WORDS

IN HER WORDS

Marie Rose Delorme Smith—Pioneer, Homesteader, Métis Matriarch

DORIS JEANNE MACKINNON AND
MARIE ROSE DELORME SMITH

FOREWORD BY DONALD MCCARGAR

HERITAGE

Heritage House Publishing Company Ltd.
heritagehouse.ca

Cataloguing information available from Library and Archives Canada

978-1-77203-520-9 (paperback)
978-1-77203-521-6 (e-book)

Edited by Crystal Gail Fraser
Proofread by Nandini Thaker
Cover design by Setareh Ashrafologhalai
Interior design and typesetting by Jacqui Thomas
Cover photograph courtesy of Shirley-Mae and Donald McCargar
Beadwork on cover and title page by Vicki Fraser,
Four Sisters Métis Beadwork (@4sistersmetisbeadwork)

The interior of this book was produced on 100% post-consumer recycled paper, processed chlorine free, and printed with vegetable-based inks.

Heritage House gratefully acknowledges that the land on which we live and work is within the traditional territories of the lək̓ʷəŋən (Esquimalt and Songhees), Malahat, Pacheedaht, Scia'new, T'Sou-ke, and W̱SÁNEĆ (Pauquachin, Tsartlip, Tsawout, Tseycum) Peoples.

We acknowledge the financial support of the Government of Canada through the Canada Book Fund (CBF) and the Canada Council for the Arts, and the Province of British Columbia through the British Columbia Arts Council and the Book Publishing Tax Credit.

Canada | Canada Council for the Arts | Conseil des arts du Canada
British Columbia | British Columbia Arts Council — An agency of the Province of British Columbia

29 28 27 26 25 1 2 3 4 5

Printed in Canada

To the Métis matriarchs in
Marie Rose Delorme Smith's family,
and particularly Shirley-Mae McCargar,
who first welcomed me
"into the family."

Contents

Foreword

∞

Reflections of a Great-Grandson

It is the summer of 2011 in the province of Alberta, Canada. As the great-grandson of Marie Rose Delorme Smith, I, Donald Walter McCargar, find myself standing on the "notorious"[1] Jughandle Ranch in southern Alberta. It is an election year, in which I have thrown my hat to be the next president for the Métis Nation of Alberta, a society struggling to be recognized as a government within Canada representing the Métis People in Alberta.

My thoughts quickly return to a time and place in the late 1800s, in what was called the North-West Territories (NWT) in the early days of Canadian confederation and western expansion.[2] My eyes focus on the current of the creek, now called Pincher Creek, that runs from the mountains in the south through Jughandle Ranch, and exit through the north.

It is clear to me why my great-grandparents chose this property in an area known for its harsh environment of wind and mountain terrain. The home quarter-section of land is located in a large swale with the flowing creek, running year-round through the property. There are large deciduous trees located next to the creek with the tops spanning across the entire sixty feet from bank to bank in a normal water flow season, creating a park-like setting, sheltered from the wind and shaded from the hot summer sun that shines 336 days a year in this area.

Marie Rose Delorme Smith made the transition as a Prairie Métis from Red River, Manitoba (formerly part of the NWT), northwest to Fort Edmonton, and ultimately south to the Pincher Creek area of what would eventually become the province of Alberta. Charlie Smith built a log cabin there in 1880. It has since vanished, but artifacts are sowed into the grass tuff. Still located on the property is the circular rock well that provided the household water. My eyes pick out a ridge located just north of the property. As I ascend to the top of the ridge, it is clear that Charlie and Marie Rose could have seen land for miles in all directions, and likely kept a look out for the herd of horses and cattle belonging to the ranchers in the area. Some historians estimate that the numbers within the herds ran into the thousands.

From that ridge, Charlie and Marie Rose would have been able to spot anyone coming into the area from miles away. The view includes the Plains to the northeast, and to the southwest, the eastern slopes of the majestic Rocky Mountains that tower over the ranch, all offering further protection from outsiders. The abundance of timber and the year-round flowing creek would have also protected Charlie and Marie Rose and the property.

As the stories have been told to me many times by family members, the location of the Jughandle Ranch was soon noted by the unruliest of men. The very true tales of the family state that Billy the Kid and the Doolittle Gangs escaped the United States, by way of a pass through the Rocky Mountains, and made their way to the Jughandle Ranch. At times, the farm was also a waypoint for family members who had been exiled from the NWT by the Canadian Army as a result of the Battle of Batoche in 1885 and were fleeing into the northern American states of North and South Dakota, Montana, Idaho, and Washington. At the same time, many found the Jughandle Ranch to be a place to rest and refreshment after being pursued on horseback. It also offered protection from the law.

Family members also noted individuals of good character, such as Father Albert Lacombe, who visited the ranch many times. Kootenai Brown and other rangers also took comfort at the ranch. Readers will learn more about these visitors in the excerpts of Marie Rose's writing in the pages that follow.

As I stand on the ridge just north of the Jughandle Ranch, I use my foot to unearth some of the sod and notice the used bullet casings and rotten tree timbers throughout the ridge. Evidence that any threat coming into the ranch was dealt with here, whether by Charlie Smith and his wranglers or by Billy the Kid and other gangs that resided at the ranch at various times.

The Jughandle Ranch spanned from east to west and consisted of the two quarter-sections with the log home located on the west quarter-section. One half-mile to the north of the property line was the other half-section of the ranch, which ran east and west, high into the rock bluffs, with sloping land into the ravines, which provided an additional source of seasonal water to the home.

My mother, Shirley-Mae Forsland, lived with her mother, Magdalene Eva Smith Forsland, and grandmother, Marie Rose Delorme Smith, at a residence at 77 Avenue and 107 Street

North-West, in Edmonton, Alberta, on the south side of the North Saskatchewan River. They enjoyed each other's company through the 1940s and 1950s, until Marie Rose's death on April 4, 1960. She had lived a long life, and was ninety-nine years old at the time of her death.

In those days, it was not uncommon to find three generations living in the same home. Security, shelter, and food were provided and protected by this way of life, whether in the city or in the more robust rural areas of the province of Alberta. Shirley-Mae lived with her mother and grandmother until she married my father, Douglas Ronald McCargar, in 1955.

Magdalene Eva passed away on February 2, 1994, at the young age of ninety-five in Westlock, Alberta. She was found sitting in a rocking chair. Her final wish was that, upon her death, her daughter Shirley-Mae should transport her remains from Westlock to her 1899 birthplace, the "notorious" Jughandle Ranch, located southwest of the current town of Pincher Creek.

Unfortunately, my mother had had a number of strokes before having an opportunity to place Magdalene Eva's remains to rest on the Jughandle Ranch.

While my mother was suffering from health issues and paralysis, she asked me to assume the position of family historian. Upon my agreement, she gave me a closet full of pictures and other family heirlooms, marked with the various names of people and the dates of their passing on the backs. Some of the artifacts included the framed pictures of Charlie Smith and Marie Rose Delorme Smith, taken in the late 1800s, which once hung on the wall in the log cabin at the Jughandle Ranch.

My mother's pictures and family heirlooms speak a thousand words and remind me of the influence she had on the man I would become.

My mother had one last request of me as she reminded me of the promise she made to her mother Magdalene Eva Smith Forsland, but was physically unable to fulfill. She asked if I could fulfill this promise. I sat quietly and looked at my mother, and realized that this was a promise of the heart that she gave to her mother, my grandmother and the daughter of Marie Rose Delorme Smith. As such, I promised to transport my grandmother's remains back to the Jughandle Ranch and provide a burial service.

I accepted my mother's request in the summer of 2009. I was running for president of the Métis Nation of Alberta and travelling across the province of Alberta meeting fellow Métis, at one point heading directly south. I was able to travel to the Jughandle Ranch and ended up crawling through a four-wire cattle fence, finding myself standing next to Pincher Creek while holding my grandmother's ashes.

I became overwhelmed with thoughts of the past three generations from a spiritual, emotional, and physical perspective, and of the three matriarchs who supported and helped to raise me. These women were Marie Rose Delorme Smith, Magdalene Eva Smith Forsland, and Shirley-Mae Forsland McCargar.

While gazing at these ranch lands, I imagined it was 1899. The incredible Jughandle Ranch was the location of many of Charlie and Marie Rose's childbirths, but one of their seventeen children stands out: this was my grandmother, who had passed many stories of her youth onto me over the past sixty-six years.

I found a location—with an energy of peace and solitude—along the creek bank to spread my grandmother's ashes. As I spread them, a wind arose and cast the ashes over the creek as the current flowed from south to north. They cascaded and spiraled in a circular form, assisted by the wind current, covering both me and the creek bed below.

As I watched and spoke words to my grandmother's spirit, the ashes dispersed into the air and landed in part at my feet on the rocks. A friend I was dating at the time assisted me and reached down to pick up a number of the rocks. With a black felt pen, we wrote the date and year of the burial on the rocks to mark the occasion. I have retained the box that held the ashes together with some of the pictures taken at the time as family heirlooms and, most importantly, one of the rocks with the burial date written on it.

As my thoughts went to Marie Rose Delorme Smith, I went from the new burial site of my grandmother on the Jughandle Ranch to Marie Rose's burial site, located in the old cemetery of the Roman Catholic Church, along Pincher Creek in the townsite. There, I found her tombstone alongside that of her husband, Charlie Smith, and some of their children.

During this time, I also wandered on a spiritual quest along the historical Métis trail of my ancestors and visited the tombstones of each generation in different locations throughout the provinces of Canada. We must look at the spiritual energy of our ancestors and how it affects our lives throughout our journeys.

On April 4, 2014, I lost the third and final matriarch who raised me. My mother, Shirley-Mae Forsland McCargar, passed away when I was in Japan with my sister, Eva Marie McCargar

Linttell. My eldest brother, Ronald Douglas McCargar, first heard the news around midnight and shared it with me. I then had to tell my sister that our mother had passed. My mother passed away on the same month and day as Marie Rose Delorme Smith—April 4.

It was clear that the spirit of Christ had prepared us for this very call that night. My sister and I commented on an experience we had earlier that day: a man approached my sister with such great momentum that I was compelled to step in to protect her. The words of this man, despite being very simple in nature, are imprinted into my memory. He stated that the Holy Spirit resides in me, and my sister answered that the Holy Spirit resides in her also. He then walked away.

We were both reassured that the Holy Spirit of God was, and is, with us. Those words were the reassurance we needed to prepare us for the grim news we received later in the evening. Today, I still grieve the loss of our mother, taken by God, but I can say that my sister and I felt peace since we had watched her suffer with paralysis for fifteen years.

As I experience different life stages, I reflect and ponder the significance of our genealogy and our spiritual connections to our forefathers and mothers. I wonder, "Are they walking with us?" I have talked to many people about their spiritual walks, stories, and life experiences. I sometimes wonder if the stories are real or imagined?

Now, at sixty-six years old, I feel like I am walking alone, spiritually, like a ghost in society. I look at my own life to answer my questions and doubts about spirituality, perhaps similar to Marie Rose. Based on what I have experienced and witnessed, I have concluded that we live in a very spiritual world and our eyes will only see what we can endure. Perhaps this was the case for Marie Rose also, as she sometimes struggled with some of the difficulties in her life.

I have reached out to other family members that have aged in this life, who offer some interesting answers. One is my cousin Henriette Forsland Douziech, who is seventy-seven years old. As we sat at her fireplace in her home, she became like a young schoolgirl wanting to share the documents and family heirlooms of our grandfather, who had married our grandmother Magdelene, Marie Rose's daughter.

It is said that upon my grandfather's arrival at the Jughandle Ranch, he saw my grandmother riding bareback on a horse to the ranch and towards her home, the log cabin. It has been said it was love at first sight for my grandfather, Donald Eveld Forsland, a young man from Sweden who was serving as a North-West Mounted Police officer at the time. I remember him as a tall, slim man who had many talents. They married and remained together until my grandfather's death.

During my visit with my cousin Henriette that day, she looked at me to see if she could trust me with her spiritual experiences related to Marie Rose. As I sat very still and watched her eyes, she described two spiritual experiences that she shared with Marie Rose. I was still, and patiently listened to her words.

Henriette described the spiritual manifestation that took place when she was the age of thirty. She said that she awoke at 3 AM, and her husband continued to sleep soundly. In her words, Henriette explained that "a young prairie woman appeared before me as though from a Star Trek movie in the transporter room. The image became clearer as the young woman in a prairie dress stood before me. Her words spoken to me were in the form of telepathy. As she communicated, she said that her name was Marie Rose and she reassured me that she would be with me through my personal life journey ahead."

Henriette experienced this spiritual manifestation again, two years later. For her, this provided reassurance that Marie Rose would be with her as she walked through her life journey.

I, too, have had many spiritual experiences. I believe I am being removed from society and walking more and more in the spiritual world. My thoughts and interaction, with society have become two different realms.

Drawing upon the knowledge of my ancestors, I believe that at birth, we receive over fourteen generations of DNA and that we can see with spiritual eyes in this realm while on earth.

I understand that Doris Jeanne MacKinnon, the author of this book and a previous one about Marie Rose Delorme Smith, was involved in the recent designation of Marie Rose as a person of national historic significance by Parks Canada. I ask all readers to engage with the rest of this book, which details the memoirs and diaries of Marie Rose Delorme Smith. In her words, we learn about the significance of her contributions to the Prairie West and to the Métis community.

Donald McCargar
Great-Grandson of Marie Rose Delorme Smith
May 2025

Introduction

IN 2023, *THE DICTIONARY OF CANADIAN BIOGRAPHY* asked me to write the entry on Marie Rose Delorme Smith. The renewed interest in Marie Rose's life story was, no doubt, inspired by Parks Canada's 2022 designation of Marie Rose as a person of national historic significance. According to the text that supports that designation, "Smith exemplified the leadership of a Métis woman . . . she successfully ran her family's ranch and established a small cottage industry in a pioneer town, while still continuing her Métis culture and skills by serving as a medicine woman and midwife." Also of note in the designation is that Marie Rose owned property at a time "when few Euro-Canadian women, and even fewer Indigenous women, were able to do so. As an author, she is a rare example of a Métis chronicler of the roles of Métis women during the fur trade, buffalo hunting, and homesteading periods, and of the cultural changes on the prairies."[1] Indeed, Marie Rose was a pioneer and a rare example of a homesteading woman who wrote about her experiences as one of the first settlers on the southern Prairies.

Marie Rose Delorme Smith's story begins when she was a young girl, born in 1861 in the Red River area of what is now Manitoba. She was a daughter of a family that had been fur traders for generations. Her great-grandfather was Urbain Delorme Sr., known as "le Chef des Prairies," as he assumed a prominent role in both the fur trade and in the community of Red River. Delorme Sr. was recognized by his contemporaries not only for his ability to lead the buffalo hunts, but for his friendship with the man who many regarded as the "Warden of the Plains," Cuthbert Grant, the founder of the community known as St. François Xavier[2] and the first founder of the Métis Nation. Delorme Sr. was active in the leadership of the Red River area, and his two sons, Norbert and Joseph, served as soldiers in Louis Riel's army, which challenged the encroachment of Métis lands by the central Canadian government and incoming settlers. Marie Rose's father, also named Urbain Delorme, may well have served alongside his brothers had he not been killed in a horse accident prior to the fighting in the Red River.

After Marie Rose's father passed away, her mother used the family funds to enroll Marie Rose and her sister Eliza in the convent school in St. Boniface, operated by the order of Grey Nuns. While her daughters were in the convent school, Marie Rose's mother married again, to a Métis man named Cuthbert Gervais, and they continued to traverse the plains, hunting, trading, and freighting. After approximately four years at the convent, Marie Rose and her sister joined her family to continue their traditional lifestyle. Based on her writing, Marie Rose very much enjoyed her family's seasonal work and was accustomed to the expectations of young girls travelling across the plains with their Métis family brigades. It was not long after Marie Rose had rejoined her family when they encountered a robe and whiskey trader, Charlie Smith.

Some seventeen years older than the sixteen-year-old Marie Rose, Charlie soon recognized that Marie Rose would make a suitable partner. As the fur trade was on the verge of transitioning to a more sedentary and agriculturally based economy, Charlie would have recognized that the skills and knowledge that Marie Rose possessed would be of value to him. Marie Rose could read and write in French and English, as well as speak a fur trade language, Cree. She also had learned many of the traditional skills "at her mother's knee," so would have been adept at establishing a homestead on the open Prairie where new settlers would soon arrive.

Not long after meeting, an arrangement was made between Marie Rose's mother and Charlie Smith, in which Charlie paid fifty dollars for this young bride. Arrangements like this were not uncommon during the fur trade era and could be beneficial to both European traders and Indigenous Peoples. For Marie Rose, this was an event that she described as frightening and uncomfortable. Nonetheless, the arrangement was well-serving for both Charlie Smith and Marie Rose's mother, who recognized that establishing a connection with a trader who appeared to be of some wealth would benefit both her daughter and her family network. Marie Rose took comfort in the fact that her mother, stepfather, and siblings travelled with them for the first year of her marriage, and they eventually settled near Marie Rose and Charlie's home in the Pincher Creek area of what would later become the province of Alberta.

Marie Rose wrote about "following the treaties," a practice that many traders assumed after Indigenous Peoples signed treaties with the incoming government. Subsequently, Marie Rose and Charlie amassed enough money to travel to

Montana. There, they gathered a herd of cattle, which they drove back to southern Alberta to establish their Jughandle Ranch. It was on this ranch where Marie Rose birthed seventeen children and established herself as a family matriarch and one of the earliest pioneers of southern Alberta. Proud of her accomplishments, Marie Rose recorded many of her experiences and those of her growing community of networks. She listed among her neighbours and friends Father Albert Lacombe, who established a hermitage in the community of Pincher Creek; Colonel James MacLeod, a North-West Mounted Police officer who helped negotiate Treaty 7; Kootenai (John George) Brown, the man who became the first park ranger of Waterton Lakes National Park; and Sir Lionel Brooke, a British remittance man who spent his final years in Marie Rose's boarding house in Pincher Creek.

The boarding house was a home for which Marie Rose negotiated the purchase from the Roman Catholic Church when she had started to handle much of the ranch transactions as Charlie aged and eventually passed away in 1914. Charlie had always continued his somewhat nomadic lifestyle, being often away from home for extended periods of time, either hunting, trading, or escorting newcomers across the Prairies. Charlie's time away meant that Marie Rose grew to depend on her own survival skills as she cared for her growing family. In fact, Marie Rose proudly referred to herself as the "Queen of the Jughandle" while others also called her "Buckskin Mary." She also established a small cottage industry, in which she made buckskin clothing and tents for companies such as the Canadian Pacific Railway.

After Charlie passed away, Marie Rose moved her family into the boarding house in Pincher Creek, where she also served as a midwife and medicine woman. At times leaving her daughters to tend to the house, Marie Rose staked a second homestead, spending weeks working on the land. It is unclear what became of this second homestead, but we know that the first homestead, the Jughandle Ranch that she and Charlie established together, was not of much material worth by the time Charlie died. There was a time that family members believed Charlie and Marie Rose had amassed a substantial estate, with large numbers of cattle and racehorses. However, by the time of Charlie's death, Marie Rose's neighbours had to come to her aid to prove her ownership of the Jughandle, as it appears that the paperwork had not been finalized while Charlie was alive. Marie Rose once observed that there was not much left "after the mortgage companies got theirs."

Marie Rose lived a full life as a mother, businessperson, rancher, homesteader, medicine woman, and active community member, and, at the same time, she was writing. It is unclear when she wrote most of her manuscripts, but there is a sense that she wrote mostly from memory. In her manuscripts, Marie Rose shared stories of the customs of the Métis and First Nations peoples, as well as recorded the stories of many of the newcomers who would form part of her new community of connections in southern Alberta. There is some indication that Marie Rose sought to have her manuscripts published as a book, though unsuccessfully. However, Marie Rose was successful in having a series of articles published in a Prairie periodical, *Canadian Cattlemen*. Living a long life, until the age of ninety-nine, Marie Rose grieved the deaths of twelve of her children. In her later life, she spent her time with family either in Lethbridge or Edmonton.

Despite never having lived alone, Marie Rose noted several times in her personal papers that she was "alone in this world." This may have been because she grieved many losses. Despite this, there is a sense throughout Marie Rose's documents that she was at peace, proud of her accomplishments as a Métis matriarch and homesteading pioneer. Indeed, her community also recognized these accomplishments. Marie Rose's visits to Lethbridge, as she aged, were often noted in the local newspaper, and, when she passed away, she was recognized as a "pioneer" of southern Alberta. At the time of her death, in 1960, it was unusual for a newspaper to recognize the death of a Métis woman. Marie Rose, indeed, was an important Métis woman who lived during the fur trade era and witnessed the transformation of the Prairies. Even so, she always relied on her Métis culture and family network to establish herself as a chronicler of Prairie history.

Marie Rose was complex. She was astute and was hesitant to share her Métis identity fully and publicly. At the same time, she recognized that she lived during a time when racist attitudes towards Indigenous Peoples were widespread. Her recognition of the southern Alberta realities, where she lived, was evident in the instances of disturbing racism that appear in her manuscripts. In some ways, these violations of racism demonstrate the difficulties that Marie Rose encountered and, no doubt, internalized as she sought to establish herself as a good-standing community member and pioneer in Pincher Creek. As a writer working with Marie Rose's manuscripts, I've often wondered how to best engage with these accounts of racism. When Marie Rose was writing in the early 1900s, her audience was primarily non-Indigenous readers. That audience would not have been as friendly to or appreciative of Indigenous voices as we are today. Regardless, Marie Rose's manuscripts are a wonderful representation of the voice of a complex Métis woman who felt compelled to marry a whiskey trader seventeen years her senior. She also felt as though she could not transparently write about her Indigenous experiences as a Métis woman. Yet, her manuscripts undoubtedly confirm, time and time again, that Marie Rose owned her Métis identity and culture.

When I first began to walk alongside some of Marie Rose Delorme Smith's family members in the early 2000s, scholars and the public knew very little about Marie Rose. This was despite the fact that, shortly after her death in 1960, Marie Rose's family had bequeathed her personal papers to what was then known as the Glenbow Museum and Archives. A few scholars referenced some of these documents in their work, including a 1977 book written by Marie Rose's granddaughter Jock Carpenter, entitled *Fifty Dollar Bride: Marie Rose Smith, A Chronicle of Métis Life in the 19th Century*.[3] While this book generated some interest, there had never been a comprehensive study of Marie Rose's writing and her life until I undertook that study and published a book in 2012. I was able to include, to a degree, Marie Rose's words, but these were short excerpts. I remained intrigued by Marie Rose's life and continued to research her writing while expanding upon my relationship with her family. This led to my 2018 book, called *Metis Pioneers: Marie Rose Delorme Smith and Isabella Clark Hardisty Lougheed*, in which I compared Marie Rose's history with that of Isabella Clark Hardisty Lougheed, an English-speaking Métis woman.[4]

As I continued to share Marie Rose's story in articles and by way of public presentations, I always felt that the published stories of Marie Rose's life had not allowed sufficient space for her own voice. These earlier publications focused on historical narrative to introduce Marie Rose's life story to both scholarly and general audiences. There was interest, and even more so when she became recognized as a person of national historic significance. Today, it is timely to fulfill Marie Rose's desire to have her words published in greater length. Marie Rose compiled most of her writing in the early twentieth century and a small amount of her work was published as articles in a prairie periodical, *Canadian Cattlemen* between the years of 1948 and 1949. That was not the full extent of her writing, and there is evidence that she was interested in adding to her published collection. This book is a culmination of my desire, and that of Marie Rose's family, to share more of her story, in her own words.

Yet, gaining a comprehensive understanding of Marie Rose Delorme Smith, in her own words, continues to present challenges. An understanding of the context of Marie Rose's life, and of the historical times and social realities in which she lived, is required for a fulsome understanding. One also needs some experience working with archival documents as Marie Rose's work comes in different formats. Letters include those written both by, and to, Marie Rose. Some texts are typed and presented in a traditional format that leads the reader to believe that the intention was publication. Some are handwritten, held together loosely in folders in the archival collections, and in some cases, those texts repeat some of the material found in the typed texts.

Although some of Marie Rose's documents appear more formal than others, all reflect a consciousness of narrative technique, which often portrays the author's thoughts and feelings as they naturally occur. Her words were not recorded in a structured way that would reflect an intent to publish, but, rather, they were an expression of thoughts as they occurred. These documents present more like a diary. Marie Rose recognized her life experiences as worthy of recording so that her memories would never be lost. There is also evidence that she produced many of her texts after significant time had passed. These are memories far removed from her lived experiences. In addition to Marie Rose's diary-like writings, there are two short pieces that present as historical fiction with content deviating from recorded events. The presentation of Marie Rose's documents, as they are found in a public archive, lend themselves to editorial introductions as a way to provide historical and current context with the intent that readers might appreciate the significant contributions made by Marie Rose to the Prairie West and to Métis history.

When engaging with Marie Rose's documents, especially those that were in her own words, it is clear that she was a racialized woman navigating her survival in a world that was much different than what she experienced during her childhood, when she traversed the Plains with her Métis family. When she was a child, the Métis enjoyed a life as "people who owned themselves." They were determined to govern themselves and protect their distinct identity and participation in the fur trade economy. Marie Rose knew her Métis ancestors as community leaders who were proud of their identity. She understood her father to be a man of some material wealth who had left his financial estate in the care of the Roman Catholic clergy. Marie Rose occasionally accessed this money after she was married.

While in their wintering camp on the Prairies, Marie Rose and her family encountered Charlie Smith, the man who would become her husband. At this time, Métis traditional ways of life were changing drastically. Charlie was of non-Indigenous descent, and there is some indication that he was a trader of material wealth. While Marie Rose feared her arranged marriage to Charlie, she would also have come to recognize that the union would result in her family's growing network and social status, especially after the couple settled as early pioneers in southern Alberta. Marie Rose also clearly sought to expand her own network by forging relationships with the increasing number of non-Indigenous settlers who were arriving in Alberta. While a racialized woman, Marie Rose was nonetheless a woman who was able to build a position of importance as a pioneer in her community.

Relying upon the education that she received while at a Roman Catholic convent, Marie Rose recognized that her education afforded her a place of privilege in comparison to many Indigenous women at that time. Her desire to record her memories of her life as a young Métis girl, and of her life as a pioneer and matriarch who was married to a non-Indigenous man, demonstrates her confidence in her social position. Yet, through her writing, we also see Marie Rose's awareness that, at times, she needed to distance herself from Indigenous Peoples. This likely served to solidify her social status.

To reach non-Indigenous readers, Marie Rose thought about the best way to present the characters who she wrote about. While recognizing that certain historical characters, such as John George "Kootenai" Brown, were not infallible, Marie Rose nonetheless depicted them as fascinating folk heroes. Conversely, influenced by both her own positionality and her desire to garner a wide readership, some of her descriptions of Indigenous Peoples can be shocking for their blunt racism. Yet, immediately following the description of Indigenous Peoples in a racist manner, Marie Rose often concluded with sentiments such as that "Indians are not fools. They are nature's best scholars."[5]

It is also important to remember that, while a racialized woman who sought to position herself among the non-Indigenous community leaders, Marie Rose would have internalized some of the colonial and westernized ideology that was inculcated in her at the convent in St. Boniface. This ideology was often evident in perplexing ways. Sometimes she used offensive and racist language, but a more benign example includes a story of her visits with Prairie folk character John George "Kootenai" Brown. In this instance, Marie Rose wrote that Kootenai regaled them with his rendition of the Métis song "Red River Valley," even recording the words of that song that formed part of the Métis culture of her youth. At the same time, Marie Rose wrote that she accompanied Kootenai on the "violin." The fiddle was more common to Métis culture, while the violin is better known for its rendition of more classical tunes than those typically enjoyed by the Métis at that time.

In their edited collection *Recollecting: Lives of Aboriginal Women of the Canadian Northwest and Borderlands*, Sarah Carter and Patricia A. McCormack note that encountering passages about Indigenous women in the archives is "exciting, rewarding—and frustrating." It is frustrating because on these rare and often brief discoveries of documents about Indigenous women, they only provide "glimpses of emotions and bonds to place . . . they leave us wanting to know more."[6] In order to learn more, the scope of inquiry must expand to include oral histories, material culture, letters, diaries, and memoirs. Carter and McCormack note that "Aboriginal women challenged and crossed borders and boundaries, real and imagined."[7] Indigenous women often did not leave a written record of their experiences. Since the documents arrived at the Glenbow Museum and Archives, Marie Rose's documents have been accessed by researchers and some of her extended family network.

Having left significant written records, Marie Rose crossed those boundaries. Yet, questions about her work remain. Take her papers, for example. Donated to a public archive in the 1960s by family, there is no way of knowing how many family members (including Marie Rose herself) read, handled, moved, and re-organized those documents. Her family expressed frustration when they reminisced about some of the material that Marie Rose had at one time, such as a book of medicinal remedies that she often relied on, which could no longer be located. There is also no way to know that the chronicles of life stories that were shared with a public archive by her family are the only written documents that Marie Rose had kept.

Archival standards have evolved, too. There were times in the past when records were more easily accessible. In the case of Marie Rose's fonds, they were stored in cardboard boxes, and could be viewed in their entirety by researchers and the public, with less monitoring than is currently the case. The lack of oversight leads to questions about the organization and breadth of her collection. In their most recent move, Marie Rose's papers were transferred to the Glenbow Western Research Centre housed at the University of Calgary, with more updated standards for access.

Until my earlier book on Marie Rose's collection, some forty years after it was donated to a public archive, Canadians knew little about her life. The "frustrations" of becoming acquainted with Marie Rose's story are diminishing as more and more family members engage with her story and share their own memories. However, Marie Rose's documents remain confusing. Often, passages are repeated in different folders and boxes, but sometimes with additions or changes. In struggling to decide what to include and to not include in this book, I considered some of those nuances of change. At times, Marie Rose intentionally included some repetition, for she would often note that "which I mentioned before in an earlier chapter," while adding further detail or sharing the story in a slightly different way.

At times, and as noted above, Marie Rose made jarring racist remarks. I am well aware of the risks of causing injury and re-igniting trauma by reproducing some of these remarks and that some may, unfortunately, choose to use these words outside of the book's context. Yet, a clear understanding of the complexity of Marie Rose's persona—as a racialized woman of some social status living on the Prairies in the late 1800s and the early 1900s—is worthy and censorship does not fit the intent of this research. Historians have established that, at various points during the fur trade and beyond, some Métis women viewed themselves as of higher status than First Nations women. Marie Rose, though, did not use the freedom of status to fully and publicly embrace her Métis identity.

In reproducing large sections of her manuscript, there are instances in which I made the decision to redact words or descriptors that are regarded as particularly offensive and hurtful to First Nations people, culture, and identity. I share these stylistic choices by using edits in closed brackets, within Marie Rose's texts reproduced here. I have also tried to keep Marie Rose's original formatting and punctuation, but for the ease of reading, I have made minor adjustments to text, throughout. These include adding spaces between words that were erroneously typed, or adding a period to the end of a sentence.

As alluded to earlier, some full-length studies have been published on Marie Rose's life.[8] However, those manuscripts, while making significant reference to Marie Rose's texts, did not include extended excerpts that would allow readers to get to know Marie Rose, the person, the pioneer, and the Métis matriarch, better, from her own perspective. Indeed, the full complexity of how Marie Rose navigated her changing world was not always fully explored or understood. This book seeks to provide readers the opportunity to engage, as fully as possible, with Marie Rose's own words as she witnessed the transformation of the Métis traditional way of life to a more sedentary lifestyle of commercialized and industrialized agriculture on the western Prairies.

Carter and McCormack note that, as scholarship about Indigenous women developed, "major debates centred around the effects of the many facets of European contact on the 'power and status' of Aboriginal women." As they argue, scholars now reject the history of the decline of power and status of Indigenous women, and they demonstrate that many Indigenous women "found imaginative and creative ways to preserve their cultures, societies, and their often complementary gender relations in the face of fur trade, missionary, and government intervention." Rather than see their status deteriorate, many Indigenous women "took advantage of post-contact opportunities."[9] One of the goals of this book, and the enduring theme, is to demonstrate that Marie Rose indeed took advantage of post-contact opportunities to establish herself as both a pioneer and a matriarch. In her own words, we are privy to the pride Marie Rose felt as she wrote about her independence, her resilience, and her ability to expand her network of connections in ways that would enable her to solidify her identity as a Métis chronicler, a small industry craftsperson, a buckskin seamstress, a mother, a midwife, a rancher, a traditional healer, a community leader, a homesteader, and a pioneer of the Prairie West. We must also appreciate that she was a complex character who, at times, perceived the realities of her society as one which held racist and misogynistic views. We must also acknowledge that she herself exhibited, at least in her writing, some of those views.

Historian Sarah Carter uncovered the family connection to Marie Rose with another aspiring writer, Ida Smith Patterson, Marie Rose's granddaughter. The daughter of Marie Rose's son Joseph Smith, Ida published *Montana Memories*, which chronicled the life of her aunt Emma Minesinger. According to Carter, Emma and Marie Rose "shared a great deal. They lived on both sides of the Canada–US border, were married at the age of sixteen, lost many children, and lived well into the twentieth century." As Carter notes, the narratives of the lives of Emma and Marie Rose "describe lives characterized by movement and change . . . Hard work was a constant in both of their lives and for both, knowledge from their Aboriginal ancestry permitted them to survive on the land. Both women sewed for a living and created beautiful beadwork designs. The memoirs of both women are imbued with nostalgia, but both are candid about the difficulties of their married lives."[10]

The candid words that Marie Rose shares in her manuscripts allow us to get to know her while we also learn about the retention of her Métis identity and culture. Her words allow us to extrapolate the knowledge that informs us about the collective, yet unique, experiences of Métis women as they navigated the transitioning world when the buffalo herds disappeared and settlers arrived on the Prairies. As importantly, Marie Rose's words provide us rare insight into the lives of the earliest pioneers who homesteaded on the southern Prairies as the fur trade was transitioning to a sedentary, agriculturally based economy.

Chapter One explores Marie Rose's memories of her time as a young girl who lived in the Red River settlement on a small plot of land for parts of the year and then traversed the Plains with her Métis family in the winter months. While writing as a married woman who had by that time raised seventeen children, Marie Rose remained enamored with this part of her life. It is during this time that she learned the skills alongside her mother that would serve her well as she grew into a matriarch of her own family and community.

In Chapter Two, we learn about Marie Rose's feelings as her family's hunting and trading brigade encountered her future husband, robe and whiskey trader Charlie Smith. As a sixteen-year-old girl, Marie Rose was ambivalent about the marriage arrangement that her mother made for her. While she protested, Marie Rose was steadfast in her assertion that she must obey both her mother and, later, her much older husband.

While Marie Rose was initially fearful about her marriage, in Chapter Three we learn about how she adjusted. She was clearly appreciative that, for the first year of her marriage, her mother and siblings continued to travel with her and Charlie. Marie Rose demonstrated her resilience and strength as she relied on skills taught to her by her family, which helped her survive as a young wife and mother.

In Chapter Four, through Marie Rose's words, we learn about her experiences of settling on the Jughandle Ranch in Pincher Creek, as well as those of her Métis community and her new community of settlers. This chapter also includes some of Marie Rose's short fictional stories, which demonstrate her creative abilities and political commentary within the safe space of fiction.

Chapter Five explores the roles that Marie Rose assumed, such as healer and midwife while also managing the ranch as Charlie continued to traverse the Plains. Marie Rose also grew to enjoy the position of matriarch of her family.

Marie Rose was widowed in 1914 and was forced to care for herself and her family for forty-six years before her death at the age of ninety-nine. In Chapter Six, we learn about some of Marie Rose's challenges, including being married to Charlie, who practiced a nomadic lifestyle and used alcohol. Marie Rose emphasizes how important her new community was in her life, especially when they came to her aid after Charlie passed away. Ever resilient and increasingly independent, Marie Rose took a second homestead while also operating a boarding house in the town of Pincher Creek.

Chapter Seven assumes a retrospective perspective, as Marie Rose's accomplishments are explored—in her own words. She viewed herself, and other fur trade descendants, as the true pioneers, the "oldtimers," who remembered the bounty of the Prairies before the arrival of settlers and fenced boundaries.

In the concluding section, as a fitting tribute to Marie Rose in summarizing her life and contributions, community members share their thoughts about this important Métis matriarch. These words serve as testimony, in their own words, as they express their gratitude for Marie Rose, who truly earned the designation of person of national historic significance.

1 — Métis Girl

I was very excited as any other little girl might be, who, at the early age of ten years, was on a winter trip over the great western plains, from the Great Lakes to the Rocky Mountains … The rising sun was just beginning its morning dance on the grey-white waters of the Assiniboine River, as my father, Urbain Delorme, with all his household sat down to the early morning meal.[1]

WRITING FROM MEMORY, MARIE ROSE DEMONSTRATES A metaphorical writing style that draws the reader in. We sense the anticipation that the young girl feels as her family embarks on a traditional and cyclical life of the Métis on the western plains. The kin group of the Delorme family, on this occasion led by Marie Rose's father Urbain Delorme, would very likely at this time have included several of Marie Rose's uncles, aunts, and cousins. Marie Rose does not mention if her grandfather, Urbain Delorme Sr., "le Chef des Prairies," would join them.[2] Even so, depending on the time of year and season, the brigade could number in the hundreds, especially when buffalo herds were plentiful.

In the excerpt below, Marie Rose describes traditional Métis life on the trails. While most of her writing is undated, this text suggests that she is writing in June of 1938. Thus, Marie Rose would have been seventy-eight years old. She was reflecting on her days as a young girl travelling with her family as part of a larger brigade. She describes, in detail, the work performed by every member of the family. Here, we also see some of her subtle political commentary, as well as her flair for the dramatic. As an example, she writes that the "French missionary priests" were "burning with zeal to convert the heathen."[3]

> I was quite young when my father died. I can just remember like a dream.
>
> ---
>
> Into this primeval land, with its innumerable leagues of prairies, lakes and forest, the first white men to venture were the French missionary priests, burning with zeal to convert the heathen, and the fur traders who speedily saw its potentialities for wealth. The fur trade really was the pioneer of civilization in the northwest. As the daring voyageurs pushed further and further inland they established forts which served as centres for barter with the Indians,[4] and when in time the two great companies, the Hudson's Bay Company and the great North West Company, entered the field, the wild lone land was still a wilderness.
>
> My father was a fur trader amongst the Indians of the Plain. In his younger days he was a settler in White Horse Plain,[5] he took land west of Winnipeg, staying on the land farming on a small scale. Money wasn't coming fast enough for him, so in the spring of 1871 my father and his family would go to St. Paul, get his merchandise and come out to winter some places where the thought would be the places where the biggest camps of Indians would winter, to catch and buy furs, &&c. He had about

forty red river carts all loaded, a covered democrat for mother and children, about seventy-five head of horses. He was a clever man, full of life, but he was cut short of his life as he died pretty young, still he made enough money to leave a fair estate for his wife and five children.

It took about three months travelling every day to reach Winnipeg, where we would dispose of the buffalo robes and furs. Oh, but that was the life! Free life, camping where there was lots of green grass, fine clear water to drink, nothing to worry or bother us. No law to meddle with us. We'd killed ducks, prairie chickens[6] and all kinds of wild game on which we mostly depended for our living. There were times when we camped near lakes to gather wild duck eggs. We'd gather them by buckets full, they were so plentiful. They were a treat. We would boil them hard so we would use them while travelling. We had no other way to pack them. Occasionally we would run on to bears, that would be a real change. Bear steak is very nice and the balance of the bear meat we would dry. We would also kill antelope, badgers, skunks, wild cats, in fact all kinds of wild animals which were good to eat. This would be some change to pemmican[7] and dried buffalo meat of which we always had lots. We also lived on wild turnips, used them for potatoes. They are nice boiled with any kind of cold meat. Once in a while, mother would make a bannock, it would be a treat to us children, even if ever so small. Our butter would be marrow of buffalo bones. They cut the bones to pieces and boil them to get the grease. It's the nicest grease I ever tasted.

You might say, how could we pack the grease so soft for travelling. Now, I will tell you, they always save the bladders from the buffaloes, they blow them and rinse them well, and fill them with grease. We also used the bladders for syringes for medical uses. Being so far away from civilization, we had to do something. We would never see a doctor from the time we would leave Winnipeg until we returned in the spring. The only one we would depend on would be the Indian doctors and wild roots in case of sickness. I tell you they were pretty good (kill or cure) we managed to live.

Wild life is a good life. Always in the open air, always breathing fresh air and a nice clean place to camp and lots of fresh green grass is wholesome. Oh, boy, give me the old time life, that's the life.

After travelling about three months, day after day, we came to a settled part of the country and the settlers ran to the road, stopped us and wanted to trade bread, butter, homemade cheese and eggs for our pemmican and dry meats. Oh, my, we sure enjoyed a change after eating only meats all winter.

Out in the wilderness we would never see a store all winter, so father and mother saved a little flour, sugar, tea and tobacco for their use. We had to be very careful how we used it. We had wild fruit for our extras. Saskatoon berries which we would dry, wild cherries which we would crush between two flat rocks and also dry. After we dried them we would use them in pemmican. Pemmican is a wholesome food. A cup of tea and a piece of pemmican makes a nice meal.

Most of the people do not know how pemmican is made: First, they cut the buffalo meat in sheets like very thin slices and hang these in rotation on regular racks made for the purpose of drying. A fire is made underneath so the smoke drives the flies away, and between the hot sun and the smoke, the meat is quickly cured. Some would do it a different way. They use stone mallets to pound dried meat to powder in a parchment skin mixing hot grease and dried berries with it and pack it all into large sacks of buffalo hide (hair on the outside). They called it taureaux[8] (French)—this was pimikan. The manna of the plains.

(Those bags are made of hide, as I said before, hair on the outside. They are made square, will hold about one hundred pounds sacks or bags, all stitched with sinew. In those days sinew was used for Thread and square needles. You readers do not know what sinew is made of, the sinews is taken from an animal, on each side of the back of the animal. It's a long strip from under the shoulder to the thigh of the animal. It's a long gricelle that they dry, removing all the meat from it. It's very fine for making thread for sewing &, even used for violin strings. It's so strong you can (strip it as fine as you like or make the strings as coarse as you like. The Hudson's Bay Co. used to pay 25 ¢ for a sinew. It was a very useful article amongst the natives and white people when they learned how to use it. The sinew must be a muscle of the back of the animal.)

Now the process of making pemmican after the meat is dried. They put it in the fire a minute or two to scorch it, and they have big skins laid out for that purpose. They put the dry meat all ready in those skins, and they have a long handle stick, and at the end of that stick they have a smaller stick tied with raw hide, and with this the men beat the meat to pieces, which has to be fine, the finer the better for pemmican. It's hard work. They have a nice grease already melted, generally it is buffalo bone grease, which is the best. This is first class pemmican. They make different grades. The women always have their bag ready made of buffalo skins & after they mix the meat, grease and berries they put it in this bag. They have a heavy stick to beat it and pack it tightly. When the pemmican is set they use an axe to cut a piece of it.

In travelling on those plains, in a way, it's not altogether a picnic. Sometime we had to travel a whole day before we would find any water. Of course we had empty oak kegs, which we always had filled with water in case of emergency. Our horses would suffer with thirst. We always had a scout riding looking for water. Sometimes it would be many, many miles before they would find a pond, then they would drive the horses to it. Now about the fuel—there is no wood on the bald prairie, the only thing for us to do was to pick buffalo chips to burn for our fire wood. Buffalo chips is the manure of the buffaloes and when dried makes a hot fire like wood. When travelling every day, day after day is always the same routine.

There is always a captain to keep order in camps especially when many families are travelling together. The captain would give orders to be on the lookout. They always ride the best running horses and carry field glasses and would go to high hills or butte to lookout. Sometime they'd sight a nice bunch of buffaloes then oh boys, there would be some excitement. You'd see the men hustle, catch their best running horses, pick the best hunters and best shots. It was a lovely sight to see these riders, whose glory it was to run and kill the buffaloes, often

> times they would be lucky enough to camp near a stream where they would remain for a few days to cure the meat and hides. The women would be excited as men, no lazy women, all would hustle, empty their carts, harness their horses and away they'd go to bring meat into the camp. Women were great workers curing the meat, making pemmican and drying hides, many buffalo robes. I remember one time, one [of] the riders got killed in running buffaloes. He was a fine young man about twenty four years old. He had killed three buffaloes and he was running for the fourth when his horse stumbled, fell and rolled over him breaking his neck. What a sad thing. He was to have been married to a young girl of seventeen. Just imagine when they brought the corpse in behind one of the riders, what emotion this poor girl went through as well as his parents. Reverend Father Lacombe was in camp so he officiated at the last rites. There were very few accidents but when a death occurred the dead were buried in the spring [when] the grove would be opened and the body would be taken to Winnipeg for burial. These were old times and they all loved one another and would not think of leaving their dead.[9]

MARIE ROSE WRITES THAT "WILD LIFE IS a good life." Through these experiences, Marie Rose learned the skills that she would later come to rely on, such as making pemmican. Her family did not have access to a store "all winter," so the Delormes had to rely on their own provisions and the country food they gathered along the way. Marie Rose also explained how they made the bags of hide, stitched together by sinew. Some of the skills that Marie Rose acquired, specifically the work in buckskin clothing, were learned from her mother. These are Métis teachings, and Métis were sometimes called the Flower Beadwork People because of their distinctive flower-design hand-crafted material cultural items. Métis beadwork combined First Nations beadwork with floral patterns that they had learned from the nuns at the Roman Catholic missions. By the 1830s, these colourful floral designs were particularly evident on products made by Métis women, like Marie Rose, from the Red River region.

Marie Rose explains that some of those "lessons learned by mother's side were later put into use, when my hand-made, buckskin gloves were much sought after by the early settlers." In the same quote, she notes that her grandfather, Urbain Delorme, left the province of Quebec for the "Great Canadian West," however this would have been her great-grandfather Francois Delorme. As noted earlier, Marie Rose's grandfather was the Métis man Urbain Delorme, born in the North West, who was known as "le Chef des Prairies" in honour of his abilities as a captain of hunting brigades. Marie Rose informs readers of the traditional lifestyle for her Métis family when they "had small farms of six chains fronting the river," concluding that they were "quite satisfied with their lot, asking only for a home, food for their families and companionship with one another."[10] As for many Métis in the Red River area, this lifestyle was to change drastically. As historian Diane Payment explains, "until the 1860s, there was no urgent need to register these riverlots or occupy them year-round."[11] However, the Métis grew increasingly concerned as more newcomers arrived. The handover of land to the Hudson's Bay Company in 1869 resulted in protests by the Métis—the very protests that Marie Rose would have referred to in the following excerpt.

Mother was a good fisherman and as she sat upon the river bank holding her line, we younger ones brought her our tiniest frogs for bait, at which the "gold eyes" anxiously snapped. Sometimes she helped us make necklaces out of the many snail shells we gathered, piercing them with a "square needle"; or from the large seed of the "white berry."

I was too young, when we lived on the farm, to be of much use about the house, but the lessons I learned by mother's side were later put into use, when my hand-made, buckskin gloves were much sought after by the early settlers of our community, from Macleod to Pincher Creek.

When my grandfather[12] left the province of Quebec for the great Canadian West, he found a settlement of Scotch half-breeds living on White Horse Plains, a few miles west of Winnipeg, and decided to cast in his lot with them.

Most of these families had small farms of six chains fronting the river and extending back as far as they cared to cultivate. They raised a few chickens and hogs; kept a cow or two; and a team of horses or oxen to plow the land and put up hay. The settlers were quite satisfied with their lot, asking only for a home, food for their families and companionship with one another.

GRANDMA VIVIA

There was one vivid character I would like to tell you about. She was an old blind woman, known to all as Grandma Vivia. She lived in a log shack with her granddaughter, Adelaide, and a little mutt of a dog named, Macoons, or Little Bear.[13] Macoons was a short-legged, curious looking animal and so hairy one could scarcely see his eyes. But what he lacked in beauty he made up in intelligence, and seemed to understand that the old woman was blind.

"Macoons," she would call and the dog then ran to her and licked her hands as much as to say, "Here I am."

Every day the trio, the old woman, the young granddaughter and Macoons, went visiting the neighbors, the girl leading her grand-mother while Macoons brought up the rear. Their only means of living was charity provided by the neighbors. As Adelaide grew to womanhood she became ashamed to be the subject of neighborly bounty, but being a very pretty girl, she was soon led to the altar, leaving the old grandmother and Macoons alone.

But still the daily tours continued and now Macoons was in front leading the old woman along the path. When meeting any obstruction, such as stick or stone, over which the old woman might stumble, Little Bear [Macoons] would stop and begin to whine and sniff until Grandma Vivia, feeling around with her cane, was able to avoid being tripped. She lived a great many years with her dog as sole companion.

As she grew older the neighbors came to call upon her bringing gifts of food and clothing. The men took turns in keeping her supplied with fuel, while the women sewed for her or made her moccasins. We girls liked to pick berries and nuts to take to her, for we felt well rewarded with her stories of her early life and many experiences she encountered on "White Horse Plains."

I think of all the tales Grandma Vivia told us, I liked best those about Sioux Indians,[14] who were always on the warpath against a different tribe. If a warrior succeeded in killing one of his enemies, he scalped him and now became a "big Nina" (Big Nina meaning Chief) for he had won honor, when he brought the scalp, mounted on a stick, to the big Pow-wow and dance.

Grandma Vivia had attended many of these pow-wow's and even at her great age she loved to demonstrate for us how the Indians danced, yelling and bending around the mounted scalp, when the blood was scarcely dried around its edge.

One morning, when one of the neighbors went to his barn, he was met by Macoons who began to pull him by his trouser leg. It wasn't difficult to know that Little Bear was in trouble. He followed the dog home and found Grandma Vivia quite ill and needing help, so carrying her to his home, he and his wife cared for her until her death.

My sister and I were often left with our grandparents when father and Mother went away on a trading expedition. Grandfather had a big house just across the church of St. Francois Xavier, a fertile district abounding in wild fruit, and grandmother prided herself on "putting up" for the winter large quanties [*sic*; quantities] of this fruit which Liza and I helped pick. I liked best to pick the wild plums which were so plentiful on the plains.

Near the river bank were many maples. In the spring, grandmother "bled" the trees and made maple syrup and sugar by boiling the sap in a vast iron pot over an outdoor fire. For a special treat, grandmother ladled some of the boiled syrup into birch-bark baskets. The French called this "cassoo." It was our special pride to help grandmother fill her well stocked cellar.

Being much younger than the rest of the family I was alternately teased and petted, and many a laugh they had at my imitations of Indian games, which they encouraged me to mimic. Their favorite amusement was to have me dance and sing the game "Change Hands." "Change Hands" was a forfeit game, a mode of amusement indulged in by all the tribes.[15] In all their games the Indians put up very high stakes.

This game required two players. First, each brought forth his forfeit; it might be a blanket, a shirt, a sack of pemmican or even much prized horses (which was represented by a stick). The two players knelt down; the one having a small, smooth bone in one clenched hand, and two similar bones in the other, had a blanket over his knees and as he sang;

Naw-moo-ya-ka-pask-in-yi-won
(Haw-haw, you can't beat me)

he brought his fists together, threw them apart, weaving his hands in circles, then up and down, now behind his back and again under the blanket—perhaps to change the position of the bones and to confuse his opponent, who must guess in which hand was hidden the one bone.

All this time he sang his song,

Naw-moo-ya-ka-pask-in-yi-won

and shouted "haw-haw," his body contortions waxed faster, the singing louder; sweat shone on the players faces and now his opponent with his forefinger outstretched clapped it down upon the hand of the first player making his choice as he sang;

Ka-pa-cik-a-tin
(I shall beat you.)

If he chose right he won three points; nine points were required for a small forfeit, more points being required for a larger one, a horse as a forfeit called for the greater number of points. So they played until one was a winner.

The spectators, squatting on the ground, were as fascinated as the players themselves, swaying back and forth and shouting "haw-haw" in unison. This was the game the older ones delighted in as I danced and sang mimicking the Indians.

Time passed swiftly and happily on White Horse Plains, until the morning I awoke sister Liza to listen to the creaking of the Red River carts and the thrill of a new life ahead of us.[16]

Above, Marie Rose transitions from talking about time with her grandmother to descriptions of traditional First Nations games. Because she wrote about memories from many years earlier, her narrative can sometimes be difficult to follow. The excerpt below includes a similar example, uninterrupted by the editorial need for linear narrative. At times, Marie Rose moved from describing the encounters that Métis had with First Nations people, to how her mother survived after her father died. After his passing, Marie Rose and her sister were enrolled in a boarding school at St. Boniface, operated by the Grey Nuns. Marie Rose's mother eventually re-married a Métis man, Cuthbert Gervais, and they resumed what Marie Rose refers to as "roaming life." Making use of her mother's "twenty carts, a democrat and thirty head of horses," the family "freighted a few years for the Hudson's Bay Company."[17] The route that Marie Rose's family used was one commonly known as the Carlton Trail, extending 1,400 kilometres between Fort Garry and Fort Edmonton, the "principal overland route in the North-West for much of the 19th Century" commonly used by Métis freighters.[18]

It was during one of these trips to the Fort Edmonton area that Marie Rose's family encountered her future husband, Charlie Smith.

> These two tribes were always at variance.
>
> Here is another instance. A party of Blackfeet,[19] about a hundred, went on the warpath to raid a Cree camp among the hills. They accomplished this and then entered a pass leading away from the raided camp only to find a second and third camp beyond it. Their presence was immediately discovered and as their only chance to escape, the Blackfeet dashed straight on to fight their way through but they found themselves in a trap as they were hemmed in a deep hollow with steep slopes, the tops of which were deeply covered in snow. Within a few minutes the Crees had closed them in and a terrible massacre began. After some seventy had been slain the Crees, their blood lust satisfied, allowed the sorry remnant of their foes escape.[20]
>
> After my father died, mother after two years of widowhood and not being very old, re-married a man by the name of Gervais. Two girls, I being one, were put in the boarding school at St. Boniface and there were still three children with mother. My father left a good estate and we children had each a share of the money and the youngest boy acquired his land in St. Francis Xavier.

Mother was to live on this land until the children were of age but my mother was used to roaming life so when she re-married they decided to freight for the Hudson's Bay Co. Mother had twenty carts, a democrat and thirty head of horses. They freighted a few years for the Hudson's Bay Co. They decided to go north to Edmonton to deliver their freight which consisted of merchandise and groceries and winter where they could trap and buy fur and buffalo. In the spring they would venture back to Winnipeg. During this time my sister and I remained in the convent at St. Boniface and I often thank my mother for the little education she was wise enough to give us. The second year after I came from school, we started out as usual on our travels we caught up to a trader by the name of Charley Smith.[21] He was a big trader, had lots of carts, horses and had four men working for him.

He had lost some of his horses so he could not go any further until he had found them and as this was bush country, it was hard to locate them. We stopped for dinner and Charley Smith invited my father and mother to his camp. He had a supply of liquor and he offered some to my people, they were both fond of their drink. Two days before we caught up to this camp my step-father had killed a young bear and Charley bought half of the bear meat from us. We camped there that night and left the next morning. When we were getting ready to hitch our horses to the cart (we, girls, always helped) I noticed Charley come around wanting to help me and talk to me but I would not answer him, I kept shy of him and he was twice as old as I was. He wanted to find out where we were to make our winter quarters. Of course, we did not know exactly until we find out where the most Indian trade would be good. Before we settled anywhere for the winter we generally roamed around the Plains to kill buffaloes for our winter meat. After three or four weeks we would then have meat enough to settle down, then we could go to a suitable place to winter. As I have told you before, there are several families together. They all work, cut logs, help each other put shacks together, plaster them with mud and hay. The windows and doors are made of parchment. The parchment is made of fawn deer skins, very thin, and makes good windows and doors; fireplace made of mud and hay and turf roofing so it did not take long to build the winter quarters. After we had again met Charley Smith, we settled by a creek, name of Tail Creek. Tail Creek comes out of Buffalo Lake north east of Edmonton. The present name of Tail Creek is Nevis. Bear Hills at that time is now known as Hobema Indian Cree Reserve.[22]

In a later excerpt, Marie Rose continues the story of meeting her future husband. She refers to the "primeval land" into which the "French Missionary Priests and fur-traders," the "pioneer of civilization in the north west . . . prepared to penetrate" using the "long train of Red River carts." Marie Rose also shared some common Métis survival strategies for traversing the Plains while hunting and trading with First Nations peoples. It was, indeed, as Marie Rose notes, the fur traders who were the "pioneers" of the North West.

While these memories are from Marie Rose's girlhood, she continued to refer to the abundance of resources on the

Prairies when she was interviewed a few years before her death. At that time, she noted that "it was beautiful country." This is the only known audio recording of Marie Rose's memories, which took place in 1957. Here, interviewer H. G. Baalim refers to Marie Rose as "Buckskin Mary."[23] This suggests that Marie Rose was recognized as someone who had retained Traditional Knowledge, as well as someone who had taken the time to chronicle her experiences so that it was important to record those experiences in an audio format. Not only had Marie Rose retained Traditional Knowledge, but at the end of the recording, she sang a few verses of "Red River Half-Breed," demonstrating a continued reference, at the age of ninety-six, to the song that was sung by many Métis in the Red River area as they traversed the "primeval land."

> **THE TRAIL**
>
> Into the primeval land, with its innumerable leagues of prairie, lakes, and forest, the first white men to venture were the French Missionary Priests and the fur-traders, who readily saw its potentialities for wealth.
>
> The fur trade, indeed, was the pioneer of civilization in the north west. As the daring voyageurs pushed further and further inland they established forts which served as centres for barter with the Indians, and even at the time the two great companies—The Hudson's Bay Company and the Great North West Company—entered the field, the wild, lone land was still a wilderness.
>
> Into this wilderness we were preparing to penetrate; but first we must go to St. Paul (east of Winnipeg) for a

season's supply of Prints, Knives, Guns, Ammunition, Axes, and oh, so many things, and when all would be packed and tied securely in the long train of Red River carts, we would begin our journey to the camps of the Indians, where father would dispose of his many wares in exchange for piles of furs, buffalo hides, bladders, grease, and the necessary pemmican with which the Indians were so plentifully supplied.

In the spring of 1871, with our train of 40 Red River carts, and the usual number of riders and 75 head of horses, led by the covered democrat, or schooner, which housed mother and us five children, we turned our course to the great prairies, seeking out the largest camps where the Indians would winter and the greatest trade in furs would take place.

There was no need to hurry. We made from eight to eleven miles a day, camping each evening where there was plenty of grass for the horses and good clear water for man and beast. There were no fences, gates or law to impede us on our way.

CAMP

After riding all day, we children were glad to get down from the wagon. We ran about looking for fuel, which consisted of bits of wood and buffalo chips. As fuel was scarce on the bald prairie there was always a race among us to see who could gather the biggest pile. It was different if we camped along a river bottom for then we could gather the dead trunks of the willow bushes.

The older ones, too, were glad to dismount. While some hurried for water, others unharnessed the horses and turned them out to graze. I wish you could have seen the poor brutes; glad to be free, they ran for the river to drink their fill, or would lie down and roll over and over.

If the day were hot we travelled early in the morning, then after the mid-day meal we let the horses rest until the evening. The men rested in the shade of the wagons or crawled under them to sleep. On such days we also travelled later in the cool of the evening. With the plentiful supply of herbage and the leisurely daily travel our horses were fast and sleek.

Wild food was abundant; when we camped near a lake we gathered wild duck eggs by the bucketsful and hard boiled them to eat while travelling. This would be a change from pemmican and dried buffalo meat of which we always had a plentiful supply.

The men shot wild ducks and prairie chickens, also antelopes, badgers, skunks and wild cat or lynx. I have often been asked to describe the taste of some of these animals. I was very fond of badger for it is very tender and tastes much like young lamb; skunk also has the taste of lamb and is nicer even than badger; but wild cat is sweeter and nicer than either, though still retaining the savor of lamb.

Sometimes we would run onto the tracks of a bear; that would be a real treat as we banqueted on bear steak. Any meat left over was dried and packed away for future meals.

We also dug wild turnips and used them as you would use potatoes, generally boiling them with meat. Sometimes we younger ones dug a white root, which grows wild and resembles a carrot in shape which also tasted much the same, eating it raw like any little girl who has just visited her mother's garden.

We had out wiener roasts, too, in those days; but in place of the sausage weiner [*sic*] we roasted gizzards and liver from the wild fowl that the men shot.

There was another animal on the prairie which wasn't so plentiful, but whose meat then as now was considered a delicacy.

I refer to the turtle.

One time I was running around playing near a cart trail and was startled by a queer strange-looking animal. As its small head reared up, and its beady eyes stared at me I was too frightened to move. I suppose the poor thing was much frightened too, but she recovered herself first and ran away. Then I saw she had been sitting upon a nest of eggs, and when I could get my breath I just stood still and screamed. The camp, as one person, came running to my aid and as I recovered from fright I gasped out, "A great-big-frog sitting on eggs." How they laughed at me, and led me away so the turtle could come back to her prairie nest.

Flour was not plentiful with us, so even a small bannock was a real treat to us children. Mother mixed flour, salt and water together, kneading the dough quite firm and shaping it into round cakes. As we carried but one frying pan the cakes of bannock were first crusted on it, then stood up against sticks in a large circle around a brightly burning fire, with mother keeping guard to turn them often so both sides might be browned evenly.

For butter we used the marrow of buffalo bones which we called "bone grease." To prepare it the bones of the animal were broken into small pieces and then

> boiled in much the same way as one renders lard today. The grease was then poured off ready for use; this grease never turned hard or set. It is the nicest grease I have ever tasted.[24]

Clearly, throughout her writing, Marie Rose felt it important to record the accounts of Métis resiliency. She also felt it important that readers understand the circumstances of her marriage to the much older robe and whiskey trader Charlie Smith.

2 —Encountering Charlie

As we neared the house, the three of us hurried real fast, and then Charlie caught hold of me, saying something. I was so frightened I knew not what his words were, but just cried out, "Yes, yes, let me go!" Where upon he kissed me and loosed his hold. I ran like a wild antelope trying to catch up with my sister and brother before they entered the house. I was still trembling with fear as we entered the door, for we girls were not allowed alone with men . . . "Oh, say Mother," I cried, "you know that white man . . . he grabbed me and began to talk . . . But first he kissed me." So ended my courting days . . . The next day, this big Norwegian trader, with his flat sleigh and jingling harness, drove up to our house. He was warmly greeted by my mother and step-father. There was much pleasant conversation between the three, and then Smith asked my mother for permission to marry me. As she looked surprised, he said, "I asked her yesterday, and she said, 'Yes.'" "But I didn't know what he was saying," I shouted at them. It made no difference. It was settled between my parents and Charlie right then, and Charlie gave my mother a present of Fifty dollars. Was I not then sold for that sum? After Charlie left, mother called me to her, "Come here, Marie Rose, you promised to marry that man." . . . I tried over and over again to explain, but it was useless . . . So I, a little girl of sixteen years, was forced into marriage with a man twenty years my senior, and of whom I knew nothing."[1]

MARIE ROSE'S WORDS, BASED ON HER MEMORIES, are poignant and telling. Agreements such as those made by Marie Rose's mother and Charlie Smith were not unusual in Indigenous communities, and they became particularly useful for European fur traders who sought to establish connections as they travelled throughout North America. There have also been recorded instances of Indigenous women seeking fur trade marriages to raise their own status in their communities. Historian Susan Sleeper-Smith argued that Indigenous women used their Roman Catholicism to expand their networks, and in effect their own status.[2] Marie Rose, though, states that she was not in favour, at least initially, of this marriage arrangement. When Marie Rose and her family met Charlie Smith, he appeared as a trader of some worth. Given that during the mid-1870s, when the fur trade was not as lucrative as it once was and the Métis were settling more permanently throughout the Western Plains, establishing a connection with Charlie would have been appealing to Marie Rose's mother. While it would also prove valuable to Marie Rose to forge this connection with Charlie, at the time, although she expressed fear, Marie Rose would not have defied her mother's wishes.

The respect for her mother was a matter of importance to Marie Rose, as she stated that it was her Mother who had "twenty Red River carts, a democrat and thirty head of horses" when she and her new husband, Cuthbert Gervais, "decided to freight for the Hudson's Bay Company." This meant that Marie Rose and her sister Liza were enrolled in the boarding school at St. Boniface operated by the Grey Nuns, where they learned to read and write in both French and English. Indeed, Marie Rose notes that she needed to "pay tribute to my mother" for enrolling her in the convent. As she writes, "even though many lonely tears were shed by her little girls, so much enriched [were] our lives with the education we received."[3] Historian Diane Payment writes of the boarding schools operated by the Grey Nuns as places "marked by loneliness and deprivation," yet, the "evangelizing and education of the 'free people' was a relatively easy task as the missionaries usually enjoyed the support of the Métis."[4]

Marie Rose and her family first met Charlie after she had finished schooling. While Marie Rose writes that her family "made camp alongside "Trail Creek," that would have been Tail Creek. This was a Métis winter settlement, also referenced as Boss Hill, in the central part of what became Alberta. The community existed between 1870 and 1879 with an estimated population of between 1,500 and 2,000 people. It served as a staging area for the Métis from as far north as Lac La Biche, Lac Ste. Anne, St. Albert, Edmonton, and east to Batoche. As a major distribution point for free traders, mule trains "extending two miles in length were used to take furs from Tail Creek des Métis to Fort Benton, Montana."[5] When the North-West Mounted Police travelled from Fort Edmonton in 1875 to visit the Tail Creek Settlement, they reported that there were 400 cabins, a community hall and timber works.[6] Today, what has been preserved of the Tail Creek Settlement is the Tail Creek Cemetery and some artifacts.

Despite the errors in referencing some community names, the following excerpt is insightful, as Marie Rose describes her knowledge of setting up the winter quarters in the mud and log "shacks." From the time of their first encounter with Charlie Smith, Marie Rose indicated that she "felt his eyes burn into mine . . . He was twice as old as

I was, yet I knew from that glance that we were destined to meet again." Whatever the attraction on Charlie's part, there can be no doubt that he recognized that Marie Rose's skills and experience would have made her an excellent partner during the transitional time on the Plains. Not only was she adept at Prairie seasonal survival, but her ability to speak many languages—including Cree, English, and French—provided critical support in Charlie's desire to establish himself as a rancher in southern Alberta. According to Marie Rose, Charlie recognized these attributes and determined from the time of the first meeting to find the camp of the "trader named Gervais . . . big outfit, got two girls just out from Convent."[7]

MY COURTSHIP AND MARRIAGE

I was still young when my father died and mother once again settled on the farm on White Horse Plains. This land was the heritage of my younger brother, though mother was to have use of the land as long as she needed it to rear her family. However, two years later she married again, and being used to life on the Trail, she and step-father, Gervais, decided to freight for the Hudson's Bay Company, taking my two brothers and baby sister with them, but entering sister Liza and me at St. Boniface boarding school.

Mother had twenty Red River carts, a democrat and thirty head of horses. Their route took them to the North West Territories as far as what is now Edmonton and after delivering their freight of merchandise and groceries, they wintered near an Indian Encampment, where they thought the trapping would be profitable.

They also bought furs and hides from the Indians and in the Spring, laden with their own precious cargo they returned to Winnipeg and rejoiced the hearts of two lonesome, homesick girls.

Four years at St. Boniface Convent[8] taught Liza and me to read and write both French and English; we already could speak the Cree tongue, and during my eighty years I have kept the three languages as my modes of expression.

But now mother thought we were old enough to help with the work on the trail, so we said good-bye to school and our good teachers. Let me pause right here to pay tribute to the memory of my mother, who, even though many lonely tears were shed by her little girls, so much enriched our lives with the education we received.

The second year, after coming out from Convent, we started as usual on our western trek. After several days of travel, we caught-up with a trader named Charlie Smith; a big, raw-boned Norweigan [*sic*], of very fair complexion. From the size of his outfit—carts and horses—we knew him to be "big trader." He had four riders working for him, but during the night several horses had strayed away, and he was now waiting until the riders found them and brought them back to camp.

Trader Smith always carried with him a good supply of liquor and, I must confess, more than his "permit" called for. Here we stopped for dinner, and afterwards Trader Smith invited my parents over to taste his liquid refreshments, with the result that we camped here all night.

Two days previously, my step-father had killed a young bear, and Charlie Smith was glad to buy half of the meat from him. He was anxious that we stay in camp until his riders returned, but since this part of the country was very bushy, my parents feared the men would be a long time in locating the animals, and it was necessary that they go with their freight.

The next morning, while Liza and I were helping to hitch the horses to the carts, Trader Smith came around and helped me with my work; talking to me he said, "You're Marie Rose?" but I wouldn't answer him, and then on glancing upward into his face, I felt his eyes burn into mine, which made me lower my gaze quickly, and thence after to try and avoid him, but he still persisted in helping me to hitch the horses to the rest of the carts.

He was twice as old as I was, yet I knew from that glance that we were destined to meet again.

"Where are you making your winter quarters," he asked father Gervais, but of course he couldn't tell him, for we never knew just where the greatest Indian camps would be and the best places for trading.

OUR WINTER HOME

As I said before, there we could be several families wintering together, so all set to work cutting logs, putting up shacks and plastering them with mud and hay. The windows and doors were of parchment, made from fawn skins, which were scraped very clean of hair and flesh and then stretched very, very thin. This made very good doors and windows.

The fire place was also made of mud and hay. Turf was used for roofing, so when all took a hand in building, it didn't take long to build the winter quarters.

After saying good-bye to Charlie Smith, we continued with our freight. Nothing of interest happened

> along the trail, so after delivering the cart loads of merchandise, and when we had shot sufficient buffalo meat, we made camp alongside "Trail Creek," that runs out of Buffalo Lake, south east of Lacombe. Today this camp site is known as the town of Nevis. We were some distance from Bear Hills which now is the Cree Indian Reserve near Hobbema.
>
> But that good-bye was not farewell to Charlie Smith. "There," he told himself, "is the girl I must have for wife." So he determined to follow after us.
>
> "See anything of a trader named Gervais?" he asked the first trail rider he met. "Big outfit, got two girls just out from Convent?"
>
> "Yes, they're on the Edmonton Trail," answered the horseman. So the Smith outfit continued on their way. Again and again the question was repeated of each rider he met, until one evening a tall, raw-boned, lanky Norweigan [*sic*] called halt to his riders and the old Bear Hills looked down on the beginning of another age old romance.[9]

Marie Rose wrote about her marriage in slightly conflicting ways. For example, above, she says that it was the "beginning of another age old romance," and, below, that Charlie was "determined to win her through love." Married life, for Marie Rose and Charlie, was not without challenges. She goes on to describe their eventual home in the Pincher Creek area, as the "beautiful little foothills of the majestic Rockies beside a small but noble little stream that gathered its waters from many cool springs." This scene, for Marie Rose, was reminiscent of her first encounter with Charlie. But then she struggled to adjust to the need to "obey" both her mother who arranged the marriage and the much older stranger who became her husband. Marie Rose wrote that Charlie loved her, and that she was treated "like a little queen." They travelled to the settlement of St. Albert to be married by the Roman Catholic Bishop Grandin. She notes that the key to her survival of her young marriage was continuing to practice the Métis tradition of travelling together as family groups. As Brenda Macdougall writes, the Métis "were the products of population movements and maintained themselves in family or kinship networks that were both inward—and outward-looking . . . the notion of building alliances through marriage was a mainstay of Métis social custom . . . that supported the development of independent and distinct Métis communities."[10]

Although Marie Rose's mother recognized the value of expanding her own family network by forging a connection to Charlie Smith, it does not suggest that Marie Rose was ever fully comfortable with the arrangement. While growing to appreciate that Charlie was determined to "win her through love," Marie Rose, writing later in life from memory, offered a warning: "Young girls, take my advice, never marry too young like I did, otherwise you'll stand the consequences."[11]

CHARLIE

A rancher in the beautiful little foothill of the majestic Rockies beside a small but noble little stream that gathered its waters from many cool springs.[12] Within that space many years elapsed so full of adventures and achievement. Some almost tragic when he had to trade with the Indians of the early 70's and 80's. Long before many whites trod the vast prairies, he travelled trading with the Indians oft times at the risk of losing his own life, marks of such encounters he carried to his grave.

Finally as the railroad was wedging its way westward, but still far in the eastern horizon, he decided to take up land to homestead. After scouring the province from north to south, he decided on a sheltered spot on the banks of Pincher Creek as it winds its way out of the foothills. To this spot he brought two hundred and fifty head of cattle. He brought these from Montana, thinking he would live a quiet, independent life with his family. He called it the old Jug Handle Ranch, originating the name. "Jug Handle" was the mark on the neck of the cattle: the loose skin was cut left hanging like a handle. To all friends or foe, strangers or neighbors were welcome day or night and no one ever left the spot hungry, Indian or white man.

When we had met Charley Smith, he was very anxious to know where we were going to winter and inquiring he finally located the place; and wintered close to us. He could not forget us, in fact many times afterwards he told me "You know, Mary, when I first met you, in my mind, I said to myself, there is a girl I must have for a wife." So that winter he eventually found our winter quarters. There was another little village about two miles from us. A priest resided there and we often went to church there. One evening my sister, Mrs. George Ness, an adopted little Sioux Indian and myself went to service. Returning home who should we meet but the trader Charley Smith in a fine flat sleigh drawn by a fine horse all decorated with sleigh bells and he passed us he said very politely "Good day, girls" but we paid no attention to him. He drove to the stable and put his horse in and walked back to meet us. He was very polite and talkative. Nearing the house, we were walking very fast, he got hold of me, said something and I was so frightened I said "Yes" so he would let me go. He kissed me and let me go and I ran like a wild antelope to catch up with my sister and the little Indian before they got to the house. We were very simple people and young girls like us did not associate with white men. When he came into the house mother noticed I was trembling and asked what was the matter. A girl as young as I, I immediately said "Mother, you know that white man, Charley Smith, he grabbed me and I don't know what he was saying, he kissed me, to let me go I said yes." That was my courting, like a flying bird. The following day who should appear in his flat sleigh and horse but Mr. Charley Smith, the big trader in all his finery. In those days a fur trader was a big man. He knocked at the door and walked in, my stepfather, Culbert Gervais, and mother greeted him. After a long talk, he asked my mother for me to marry him. Mother was rather surprised but he told her that he had asked me yesterday and I had said yes. That word "yes" was misunderstood, it was alright for Charley Smith but not for me. So it was arranged that I was to marry and Charley Smith gave a present of fifty dollars to my mother, I being an orphan girl.[13] I might as well say I was sold for fifty dollars. He being a Protestant and I being a Roman Catholic, we could not be married by the local priest so we had to go to St. Albert where the bishop resided. After Charley Smith left, mother called me to her and said "Marie Rose, that man told me that you had promised to marry him." I cried real loud and said "No, no, mother, I never did. He got hold of me, I said yes for him to let me go, not knowing what he was saying. Mother, I don't want to get married." My tears never helped me any. I tried to explain to Mother, but she said that as I had promised the man I would have to marry him. The following week preparations were made to go to Edmonton, Charley Smith furnished three sleighs and horses and he was riding. The snow was terribly deep in February, 1887. All this time my heart was broken—being so young and not knowing anything but—obedience. To the wedding. The snow was so deep it took a few days to get to St. Albert. They took great care of me and treated me like a little queen. They wrapped me in buffalo robes and gave me a driver to drive my flat sleigh but all that did not suit me. When we would camp, they had to dig snow so as to put the teepee. I would stay in the sleigh until the teepee was warm and then they would carry me in. After three days, hard travelling in deep snow, we arrived in St. Albert where I was married by his Lordship Bishop Grandin to Charley Smith, twice as old as I and he knew I was too young for him, however he loved me very much and was very patient with me. Our honeymoon was not all honey, it was more like sour grapes to me. The summer I put in, I will never forget. I would wonder away alone and cry to my heart's content. As the years rolled by I commenced to realize that I had to obey, it was a hard task for me. One consolation [was that] my parents travelled with us all summer. Through the day I would forget my troubles playing around with my sisters and brother but towards evening my heart would commence to throb. What a feeling, no one knows but myself. Young girls, take my advice, never marry too young like I did, otherwise you'll stand the consequences.

I will now explain how we happened to have a little Sioux Indian in our family. When we were travelling on the Plains those days, Sioux Indians had mostly dogs and travois to haul their belongings, perhaps there would be an odd one that would have a pony but they all travelled on foot, men, women and children. That was the way they wandered over the Plains, depending on wild game and buffalo for a living. We had arrived at a vacant camp, my father, mother and children in the democrat, ahead of the string of carts, and we found this.[14]

Additionally, some of Charlie's practices were unfamiliar—and even shocking—to Marie Rose. About his trading practices, she wrote,

> *We traded for cash or skins, some of the provisions from our loaded wagon. It was regular robbery! One pound of tea, we traded for one buffalo hide; one pound of sugar for one skin . . . Charlie had more liquor than his permit called for . . . While the police searched, Charlie buried his kegs in the water and brought back buckets of water and treated the police from the store of whiskey, to which he was entitled by his permit.*[15]

According to Marie Rose, when she and her family met Charlie Smith, he appeared as a trader of some wealth. She wrote that "from the size of his outfit—carts and horses—we knew him to be a 'big trader.' He had four riders working for him."[16]

However, the fur trading on the Prairies was changing. As Indigenous Peoples and the Dominion of Canada made treaties with each other, traders assumed a practice of "following the treaties," as Marie Rose indicated she and Charlie had done. This was especially so in Western Canada with the signing of the Numbered Treaties between 1871 and 1921. Some traders amassed significant wealth from trading with Indigenous Peoples after the signing of the treaties. For Marie Rose and Charlie, they accumulated personal wealth by way of the cattle herd they bought in Montana and bringing them to their ranch in the Pincher Creek area, where they also raised race horses. At times during their life, family members believed that the couple were "wealthy." Despite any material wealth they may have accumulated, Marie Rose and Charlie experienced a fair number of challenges. Some of these included Charlie's nomadic lifestyle and heavy drinking, but also his generosity of hospitality. She notes that, "we never seemed to be alone in those early pioneer days."[17]

Yet, Marie Rose spoke fondly of their shared home in the Pincher Creek area. She wrote that, "the country was pretty . . . others talked about being lonely, we don't know the feeling. Horses and cattle, hundreds in one herd . . . game of all kinds was plentiful." While she loved sharing details of the bountiful land where she and their family had settled, Marie Rose also elaborated on her growing network of neighbours and newcomers in the Prairie West.

OLD AUNTIE[18]

After Mr. Schoening had visited in Manitoba in the winter of /83 and /84, in the latter part of April 1884, Mr. and Mrs. F. Crook left Manitoba for Pincher Creek. They were accompanied by Messrs. F. Neuman, A Skeide, F. Schweinfurth, WM Bratke, wife and child. We came as far as Medicine Hat by train and were met there by G. Neuman with horses as we had brought two wagons from Winnipeg. Besides stoves, trunks and other effects, we brought one rooster and four hens. Mr. T. Lebel and his men left Medicine Hat at the same time that we did but they had Red River carts. We were two weeks travelling to Pincher Creek and we camped wherever we found water. One night we spent at Coalbanks, now Lethbridge, and were taken across the Belly River on a ferry. We also spent a night at Fort Macleod. Mother baked fry cakes[19] and Indians watched her doing it, some of them were only partly dressed. The next night at Lagrandeur's place. It was raining and he very kindly let us have one of his buildings to camp in. At last we arrived in Pincher Creek and the first person we saw was Old Auntie standing at her door smoking a pipe. I remember seeing only a few houses in Pincher Creek, a store, post office and two or three log cabins. There were not many people here. The police barracks was where it is now and the redcoats were respected by all.

It was about the middle of May when we arrived and we went to Mr. G. Neuman's place four miles southwest of the town. The country was pretty, a lot of grass, beautiful flowers and plenty of water and the best view of all, the mountains in the west. It was all new to us, we loved it and after all these years we still love it. Others talked about being lonely, we don't know the feeling. Horses and cattle, hundreds in one herd used to cover the prairie. Game of all kinds was plentiful.

Mr. F. Neuman and Mr. S. Skeide, who left their wives and children in Manitoba returned for them in the month of June.

That fall Mr. Schoening and the other men built a nice roomy log house 18 x 24 and we lived in that home for nearly two years when we all went to our own homes.[20]

Below, Marie Rose describes her first home as a married woman in a social setting that was increasing defined by pioneer culture. But Marie Rose had a well-established understanding of and respect for those who were well-established, or the "oldtimers." Indeed, some of her understanding would have been derived through her membership with the Southern Alberta Women's Pioneer and Old Timer Association (formed in 1922) and she was concerned with "the memory of its early pioneers" and sought to make a contribution to this memory.[21] Marie Rose considered "oldtimers" as the true pioneers: "There is a different class of people today compared to the oldtimers who were so friendly and helped one another . . . The old pioneer days were happy days and wants were few."[22] Marie Rose went on to write that "the new settlers do not realize what the oldtimer had to endure to make this country livable for them."[23] As a member of the Southern Alberta Women's Pioneer and Old Timer Association, formed in 1922, Marie Rose would have been aware of one of its primary goals to preserve and "rescue from oblivion the memory of its early pioneers." The goals of this organization may have served as inspiration for Marie Rose in recording her experiences and those of her community.[24]

BITS OF MY HOME LIFE

It was in the fall of 1880 that we decided to settle near the little stream now called Pincher Creek, which then was teaming with roaming Indians. I was then twenty years of age, twice as young as my husband, a very open-handed fellow, and everybody was welcome to our house on Jug Handle Ranch.

We lived in a long, log house, of one room, with the roof made of bark. The chinks between the logs were filled with mud. There was no flooring in the house and windows were constructed of small bits of glass.

Our furniture was such as could be home made, but we had a good stove. Our cupboard were boxes nailed to the wall and though dishes were few, food was plentiful. We had a few pictured calendars on the wall, which lent a spot of brightness to the place.

One of these calendars had a picture of two little negroes which was the cause of the following episode. Any time the mill closed down, the boys would stampede to Charlie's place and wait for the next cargo of liquor to arrive. They would lie around anywhere, in the kitchen or cut under the wagon, or any place they might fancy made a good sleeping ground.

It was during one of these holidays that Bill Lees and Lou Jewel couldn't sleep, so seeing a bucket of white wash and a brush near by, wondered to what use they could put it and immediately began to brush them over with the whitened liquid. But there was plenty of the wash left over, so going among the sleeping men, they freely whitened their companions, faces, clothes and all.[25]

We never seemed to be alone in those early, pioneer days. At any time of the day, Charlie would say, "Well, Mary, put on the potatoes, I go to catch a mess of fish." But the potatoes were scarcely peeled, ready for the pot when Charlie would return with a string of fish.

Game was plentiful, too. Often some of the boys, just stood in the doorway and shot a feast of prairie chickens or partridges.

There were no saloons here at that time, so Charlie would ride into town, and at the drug store was able to purchase Jamaica Ginger, at fifty cents a drink. Most of the families had a permit, which allowed two gallons per family, and whenever their supply came, the neighbors gathered round and the drink was shared.

Charlie, just beginning to feel good on Jamaica Ginger would say, "I am bright as some star and slick as some 'veazel.'" He always ended up by singing, "Raspberry Yam, Strawberry Yam," and then go to sleep.

Our most frequent visitors were the boys from the mill, for they knew that Charlie would treat them to Jamaica Ginger. "Anything you wish for, just holler," Charlie would say.

One time, Charlie thought he would make the boys some soup, but of course he must have his measure of fun to compensate him for his work. So seeing the greasy dish cloth on the table, he dropped it into the soup, and boiled it well.

In the afternoon, there arrived barrels of beer, a few bottles of Scotch and some Montana Bourbon Whiskey. The "white-washed" fellows awoke, angry, but soon forgot their troubles again.

Charlie called me to set the table, while he dished out the soup, and holding up the boiled dish rag yelled, "Who wants some tripe?"[26]

The words that Marie Rose chose reflect her challenges as the wife of a much older non-Indigenous man who often showed disregard for Marie Rose's discomfort resulting from his actions and words. Marie Rose had been clear that she had no option but to obey her mother, who made the marriage arrangement, and then her husband. There is a sense that she hoped her readers would understand the challenges for her, as a young wife and mother, whose words were sometimes tailored to suit an audience which would very likely share Charlie's views on women and on racial superiority.

3 — Young Married Woman

The only time I could properly feed my children was when all were asleep . . . Many, many nights, I sat on the end of my long cot, with the children lying crosswise of the bed, packed together like little sardines, watching for fear the boys might upset the lamps and burn my little ones to death, or in their stupidity wander to the bed and fall upon it and crush one that might be sleeping . . . You will wonder why I did not object to having the house full all the time . . . It was no use, Charlie was boss.[1]

BETWEEN 1878 AND 1904, MARIE ROSE BIRTHED seventeen children. Although historical accounts of Marie Rose's husband are limited, those that exist suggest that his hard-living habits would not have been approved of by the nuns of the convent in St. Boniface, where Marie Rose received her education.[2] While the nomadic lifestyle of many Indigenous Peoples meant that it was unusual for Indigenous women to give birth to seventeen children prior to contact with Europeans, the influence of the Roman Catholic clergy on the Métis often led to larger families.

Additional evidence that Marie Rose faced hardships can be found in a short piece titled "Tribulations." Although this piece is credited to "Mrs. C. Smith," it is clearly a transcript of an interview that Marie Rose gave to an unknown writer.

The writer notes, "As a rule, mammals of the human variety are transferred from this earth to a better place, unless he or she or both finish up in 'Hell Creek.' On Mrs. C. Smith the process is reversed—she first spends considerable time in 'Hell Creek.' Later on in life she takes residence in an earthly paradise."[3] While undated, the document suggests that the interview occurred when Marie Rose was seventy-two years old, about eighteen years after Charlie's death in 1914. Although Marie Rose briefly wrote about this herself, the author of this excerpt provides details that highlight both the challenges and accomplishments that Marie Rose faced. These details showcase her resilience and independence during her journey by cart across the Prairies—from southern Alberta to Winnipeg—in hopes of reuniting with her wayward husband.

TRIBULATIONS OF MRS. C. SMITH OF PINCHER CREEK ALTA. BY MRS. C. SMITH

As a rule, mammals of the human variety are transferred from this earth to a better place, unless either he or she or both finish up in "Hell Creek."

On Mrs. C. Smith the process is reversed—She first spends considerable time in "Hell Creek." Later on, in life, she takes residence in an earthly paradise.

Modern annoyances do not affect her in her late state of beatitude—They do not compare with her former trials although boisterous kids and gay parties, unmindful of her seventy two birthdays do not give her any respite, she is not a bit upset.

In 1880, on a wild site, called Pincher Creek, lousy with roaming Indians, Mrs. C. Smith, at the tender age of twenty, legitimate wife of Jug Handle Charlie, twice as old as she, was looking after him, as well as after a bunch of cayounes [*sic*; cayuses],[4] children and cattle.

Everybody knew Charlie, and what kind of life he was leading, an awful good man. Everybody was welcome to his house—There, no one ever left the place with an empty stomach—Anything you wished for! You just hollered.

He was twenty years her senior when he proposed and yet: He fell for her. She had kept shy of that tall rawbone lanky, but eventually fell through.

The consequences were not altogether pleasant.

Then, Mrs. C. Smith, known as Buckskin Mary was this queen of the Juggle Handle Ranch of which specifications are as follows:

Log House, made into just one big room, all mudded between the logs—Roof made out of bark. No flooring—Regular windows but just little bits of glass—No regular furniture—No regular beds.

They had the cook stove—Decorations consisted of old pictures they had picked up—For cupboards, they just nailed boxes on the walls—No pantry—very few dishes. No fancy ones but lots of grub though.

Charlie used to catch the fish. « Well Mary, put on the potatoes, I go and catch a mess of fish ». Before Mary got through with the potatoes, the old man would come with a big string of fish.

From the door, the "boys" would shoot the prairie chicken, any kind.

They had such a nice life—There were no saloons, no nothing—The old man would reach a drug store and buy Jamaican ginger[5]—(fifty cents a drink).

Of course people could send for a ferment: two gallons for each family. Whenever they got their two gallons, they all had invite each other and have a big drink.

Charlie, just beginning to feel good on Jamaica Ginger] would say « I am bright as some star and slick as some Veazel [*sic*; weasel] ».

When Charlie was half shot, he would say « Oh Mary never mind, God will be made king done [*sic*; kingdom] in Heaven ».

The old devil had rough ways but lots of good hearts at the last stage[6] he would say « Raspberry Jam—Strawberry Jam » and go to sleep.

One fine morning in the spring of 1882, Charlie said to Mary: « Be good, there is a boom in Winnipeg, I am going there ». Whereupon he left on a buckboard with his bed, the eats, frying pans and tea kettles.

Mary was left to run the ranch and the hired men to put in a nice garden—Remember that Winnipeg is a place which you could locate about nine hundred miles East of Pincher and that there was no train, nor mail of any kind.

The garden—stuff was growing fine but Mary thinking that Winnipeg was not far away after all, soon embarked on a Democrat with her three little boys she took five heads of gentle horses. The democrat carried also, a canvas tent, the eats, frying pans and tea kettles. Mrs McGillis and children joined the party—They also had a democrat and extra horses—Old Joe Brown the fiddler on horse back was the escort.

Every night in the tent, Joe would play some good old time tunes—One morning, Joe said « I believe there are some Indians following us up—I seen some moccasin tracks when I went after the horses ». The next morning, as the ladies were boiling the kettle, Joe came along with hobbles in his hands, saying « Our horses are gone—They cut the hobble leaving us the old brown mare ». So he went to a nearby place, got a saddlehorse and set out to Montana after the thieves. An Indian trader lent the ladies twenty dollars.

One month later, Joe turned up with three of Mary's horses, four of Mrs. McGillis and his own—They were having a good sleep, over that while homesick Charlie, a few miles north of the tents was fussing[7] them on his way back to Pincher. You can well imagine, Mary's horses staying a neighing emcent[8] at some particular time of the night, the silly beasts, heads northwards, scratching the ground—Nobody heard them though.

Instead of taking timely information from a gentle horse, the caravan had gone on quietly to get it one month too late from a gentleman in Winnipeg.

Indeed, it made no difference how bad the mix up was since it afforded Mrs. C. Smith the opportunity of bringing to Pincher, Charlie's Mah in Law. This particular old lady had no coins nor bunions on her feet as she was always wearing moccasins, neither had she any false teeth in her head as she was mostly feasting on galette and pemmican.

Charlie, at the Ranch, was almost crazy about his wife and children, thinking that the Indians had murdered them. He kept riding around Pincher until he detected a couple of tents at a distance—Approaching the tents, he saw some moccasin tracks. That sent him in the war path.

> You know the rest. The old lady and her daughter got him and hanged on to him—The Indians had got him.
>
> The smell of Queen Mary's cooking had attracted the boys working at the sawmill, up the creek—They made themselves comfortable, feeling quite at home in the one big room—« Anything you wish for, you just holler » would yell Charlie.[9]

Above, Marie Rose referred to herself as "Queen of the Jughandle," demonstrating her growing competence and independence. When Charlie returned home from one of his many trips across the Prairies, after having been away most of the summer, he found that his wife and children were not home and he had no idea where they were and if, in fact, they would return. According to Marie Rose, Charlie was beside himself when she did return. Charlie recognized Marie Rose's value as a partner, given her Métis experiences of living a traditional lifestyle and following the buffalo herds across the Plains. In a chapter in *Eighty Years on the Plains,* entitled "Home Industries," Marie Rose described her buffalo skills. She called it the "most important industry . . . the making of pemmican." She continued to make pemmican into her later years, with her granddaughter Shirley-Mae McCargar, in Edmonton.[10] In the excerpt below, Marie Rose describes, with extensive details, what some called "Pimikan." She also provides details of working by the light provided by "rags soaked in buffalo grease" and, later, candles that they made, which enabled her to continue making the traditional clothing.

While living in Teepees we didn't need lamps, as the fire in the middle of the floor gave sufficient light; but when we changed to canvas tents we had to have a different kind of light, so the buffalo grease lamp came into use.

This lamp consisted of a tightly-twisted rag of any kind soaked in buffalo grease and then with one end lying in a shallow dish of the same fat, we lighted the opposite end. The grease kept feeding through the rag and it made plenty of light by which to work.

As the years went by and we spent our winters in log huts, we required greater illumination for the long winter nights, so we used candles which we made ourselves. First we ripped seamless sacks, took the strings thus ravelled and twisted them together. Then into a deep kettle of melted buffalo fat, floating on water, we dipped the twisted string, in and out, in and out, letting the fat harden between each dip and gathering more grease with each immersion until at last the candle was the thickness we required. It was a slow process.

With the coming of the settlers, coal oil lamps were introduced to us, but we would not use them as we were afraid they would explode, and moreover lamps were costly to buy. But as time went on we became used to them.

We also made our soap. There were, along the various streams, several places known as Poplar Point, and near one of these we made camp. The men at once began to cut down the trees and make huge fires, keeping them burning both day and night; the ashes thus obtained were put into larger sacks.

Water was then boiled in great copper kettles, and while still boiling, the contents of the sacks were emptied into it and stirred over and over again, until a strong liquid or lye was formed. The liquid was ladled into open gunny sacks and held over the kettle to drain; this again was mixed with buffalo grease and again boiled. It made excellent soap.

Our most important industry was the making of pemmican. First I will tell you how *second grade* pemmican was prepared. Buffalo meat was cut into very thin slices or sheets, and then hung up to dry on rows of racks made for this purpose. A fire was made underneath, so no flies would bother the meat while it was being smoked for curing and also being dried by the heat of the fire and the hot prairie sun.

When dry, stone mallets were used to pound the meat to powder in a parchment and when fine enough it was mixed with hot grease and dried berries. This mixture was then packed in large sacks of buffalo hide. Sometimes, for lack of time, the hair was left on the outside of the hide; the French called this Taureaux, others called it Pimikan, The Manna of the Plains.

To make *first grade* pemmican, the meat was first dried, then put into the fire for a minute or two to scorch. Big skins were laid out and the slightly scorched meat was placed on them and was ready to be pounded with a flail. The men beat it again and again, for the finer it was the better it would be for making first class pemmican. The beating was done by the men as it was too hard for the women to do. Hot buffalo grease was then melted and mixed with the powdered meat; so you see the difference between

> the grades of pemmican was the degree of fineness into which the meat was pounded.
>
> It was the women's work to have the bags of buffalo skins ready. Just before this high grade pemmican was packed the dried and crushed berries were mixed into it, and then with a heavy stick it was beaten into the bag, packed tightly and sewn in. After the pemmican was set an axe was used to get a piece to eat.
>
> The sacks were square in shape and held about one hundred pounds each. They were stitched with sinew, using a square needle. (A square needle is not as its name implies, but is three sided in shape with a very sharp point, the thread end being round like an ordinary sewing needle. The razor-like edges of the needle, along the sides, cut the skin to allow for the passage of the sinew.) This sinew is taken from each side of the back of the animal. It is a long strip stretching from under the shoulder to the thigh. It is really a gristle that is scraped clear of all meat and then dried. It is so strong and tough, that it can be split.[11]

As evidenced in the excerpt, Marie Rose relied on her Métis culture and family to establish herself as a matriarch. At one point, Marie Rose was quite proud of her ability to provide for her family. Marie Rose was certain that readers would "be interested to know about the Red River carts," so she explained their construction and importance as a critical tool that supported Métis traditional lifestyles. Marie Rose goes on to explain women's work during buffalo hunts, work that she continued as a young married woman when she established her small cottage industry. This work earned her the name "Buckskin Mary," in recognition of the beaded buckskin clothing that she made for her family and for sale to tourists and work crews. She noted though, that "perhaps the greatest work among the women was the tanning of hides."[12] It was this work that not only provided clothing for family networks, but also served as an important source of income for Métis women. Years of experience, both that of her mother and her own, as well as her connections in the Indigenous community, meant that Marie Rose had knowledge of the best sources for her hides. After settling in the Pincher Creek area, Marie Rose expressed a preference for certain tanning methods: "In making my buckskin gloves, slippers and other garments, I send to the Mission House of the Kootenay Indians, near Cranbrook, B.C., as I prefer their form of tanning to others."[13]

As Sarah Carter and others have noted, women's handiwork "was an important aspect" of their lives and the labour that was critical to the survival of their families and to the retention of their cultural identities. Carter argues that "a woman's competence in this domain and her artistic abilities affected her personal status."[14] Their work not only covered the labor costs of the fur trade but also gave Indigenous women a sense of independence both during and after that period.

BEADWORK: RED RIVER CART

> You will be interested to know about the Red River carts in which the traders used to carry their merchandise into the interior of the country and then to bring their furs out. The noise of these carts could be heard miles away in the prairie stillness. They were made entirely of wood-oak from Winnipeg and rawhide no iron at

all being used. One often wondered if it were possible for them to hold together but the rawhide thongs were strong and they always finished their journey. With a small amount of repairing they were soon ready for the next trip. Traders always carried extra spokes to mend the carts if needed on the trail.

Perhaps the greatest work among the women was the tanning of the hides. After the skin of the animal was well scraped of all meat, it was stretched and dried. Later it was immersed in the river or lake for a few days of all hair. There were two different kinds of scrapers used; first I draw the knife, and second one of the animal's ribs, the latter being the better to use as it did the work more evenly.

The best scraping was done by following the "grain" of the hide. It made the finished work of softer texture and an evener thickness. (Scraping crosswise of the grain made the leather shiny and crusty.)

As the neck of the animal was thicker than the other parts of the hide, the scraping began at the neck end of the pelt and worked downward. The fingers of a good tanner were very sensitive in detecting any unevenness in her work and knew just the right pressure to bear to obtain an even thickness.

Now the finished product was white and felt velvety, but the women did not stop here, for if a rain storm caught them with the white leather garments, they would turn hard when dry. So the next step was smoking the leather, which turned it a rich light tan, and would keep its softness.

(In making my buckskin gloves, slippers and other garments, I send to the Mission House of the Kootenay

Indians, near Cranbrook, B.C., as I prefer their form of tanning to any others.)

Though we can now buy glass beads in almost any shade for trimming buckskin garments, the Indians in earlier days used porcupine quills which they dyed with natural juices, and had quite a gift for fanciful patterns. They often paid dearly for white horse tail, which they also dyed and used for trimming moccasins or making horse hair ornaments.

Young mothers, too, when on the trail, vied with one another in seeing who could make the prettiest Ti-ki-na-kan (baby beaded bag) which is the cradle of the papoose and is strapped to the mother's back when travelling. We were just as proud to "show off" our bead work on the baby bag as you are to display your knitting or embroidery.

We made our own shoes or moccasins, beading in pretty designs the ones we wore for holiday wear. Long hours were spent beading the front of the vests, the cuffs of coats; and the lad with a nicely beaded buckskin shirt was proud indeed. Solid beaded belts were quite common among the braves; and fringed, beautifully beaded trappings for the horses lent a distinguished look to a many a mounted chief.

This beaded work was once laid upon the graves of the Indians only to be filched by passing white men. Now the much-prized work is handed down from father to son. The Calgary Stampede, each year offers special prizes to the best decorated [Indigenous men and women] on horse back, the beaded harness aiding in the judges' decision. It would be difficult, indeed, to match the wonderful display shown there.

Bead work is a tedious process, for each bead has a stitch of its own. Much of this work I learned from my mother, and I enjoy making original designs on all my buckskin work.

Here is a picture of Miss Sharpe wearing a complete suit of buckskin which I made myself. Note the beaded head band, the beaded yoke on the buckskin blouse and beaded moccasins. The picture does not show very well the bead work along the sides of the trousers. This suit was made for the checking girl at the hotel in Waterton Lake Park at the request of the management.[15]

Do you remember our old "quilting bees"? We must have adopted the idea from the elderly [women], who held "Teepee Bees."[16]

These accounts speak to Marie Rose's important contributions to the family economy. As Marie Rose notes in the following excerpt, fifteen of her seventeen children were born on the Jughandle Ranch near Pincher Creek. This was common at the time, as many pioneer settlers on the Prairies relied on the help of Indigenous midwives.[17] While Charlie did not "beat her into submission" as per the advice he had reportedly been given when they were first married,[18] he grew to appreciate Marie Rose's skills and her independence. In another version of a trip, Marie Rose relates her experiences when Charlie left her and the children on the Jughandle Ranch for the summer while he travelled to Winnipeg.

Growing tired of waiting for Charlie to return, Marie Rose undertook the journey across the Prairies herself, with her children, a neighbour and "an elderly man" who was a "good fiddler, [so] it made a pleasant addition to our party." It was quite a journey, as the traveling party encountered challenges. Their horses were stolen and they had to camp at Fort Walsh until their elderly companion recovered the horses, which took longer than a month. They then traded their carts for train tickets on the newly constructed rail lines. Marie Rose and her sister, who had joined the travelers in Batoche, finally arrived in Winnipeg. Accessing the inheritance left by their father, whose estate was managed by the Roman Catholic Bishop Alexandre-Antonin Taché, Marie Rose was able to re-equip herself for the journey back to southern Alberta. Writing from memory years later, Marie Rose did not doubt her ability to find her way back home and ensure safety for her children as she traveled. While the excerpt below focuses primarily on Marie Rose's journey to Winnipeg and back, the first few lines speak to the fear that Marie Rose experienced when she first realized that she had no options but to marry a stranger who was much older than her.

> "Beat her into submission," was the advice given to my husband. But Charlie was patient and determined to win me through love.
>
> Finally when we settled on the ranch at Pincher Creek, we had two boys (one born in Montana and one in Winnipeg) and Jug Handle Ranch was the birth place of our other fifteen children. This family of seventeen children, was a heavy responsibility for which to provide food, clothing, medicine—with the nearest doctor, for many years being no nearer than [Fort] Macleod, 30 miles away.

Shortly after settling on the ranch, in fact in 1882, there was a boom in real estate in Winnipeg. We had, working for us that year, a man named Jack Bruce, a Scotchman. He had property in Winnipeg and when the word spread about the boom, he offered Charlie One Thousand Dollars to take him there. That was on April tenth.

The snow was very deep, but they took the buckboard to carry their bedding and cooking utensils, which consisted of a frying pan and teakettle. One horse drew this light load, while two others were tied behind. They were gone all summer, and I was left behind with my three boys and a hired man to look after the cattle and horses. He was a good worker and planted for us a good sized garden.

But it was lonesome with only my small children, and when the hired man began to get "fresh" and wanted to kiss me, I knew I would rather suffer hardships on the trail than be subjected to the ugly attentions of this hireling.

Thus I made ready for the trip, heading toward Winnipeg, with a covered democrat, five head of horses, a tent, the necessary clothing and food enough to last until I would meet my husband, some where on his route back.

But the children and I were not alone. A neighbor, Mrs. McGilliss, with her son and daughter were going to the Cypress Hills and we went along together. There was also an elderly man, Joe Brown, also starting for Winnipeg, as he was a good fiddler, it made a pleasant addition to our party.

Everything went well for about a week, when one morning Joe announce, "I believe there are some Indians following us. I saw moccasin tracks when I went after the horses this morning."

We were now near Fort Walsh, so we made an early camp, that evening in order that we might tidy ourselves before going to visit our friends at the Fort.

By morning, excitement ran through our little company as we prepared to set out for the Fort. Mrs. McGilliss boiled the kettle while Joe went after the horses. Then came our big disappointment, for we saw Joe returning, carrying with him the hobbles, which had been cut from our horses feet. The Indians had made off with all the animals except Molly, an old brown mare. Joe owned but one saddle horse, a beautiful roan mare, that was to him like an only child, so he vowed vengeance to the thieving Red Skins. It was a sad group that sat down to breakfast.

It was an angry Joe Brown who rode into Fort Walsh, that morning to hire horses that we might use to move us into town. After seeing us settled at the Fort, Joe secured a saddle pony and announced, "You'll not see me coming back until I'm driving every critter before me, that them hoss thieves stole."

Day by day we waited, looking toward the Montana border for Joe to return. Our food supply was getting scarce, and I had brought but little cash with me. A month we waited, a month watching the sky lines for our rider's return.

While to the south, on a lower road, there drove a man in a buckboard, his spirits rising, for he thought he would soon see his wife and three babies. What a happy reunion he looked forward to, little realizing that a few miles across country was a little family on its way to meet him on the Winnipeg trail.

We had no mail, by which we could communicate with one another, so at the end of the month, when Joe returned, bringing with him his own beautiful horse, three of mine and four of Mrs. McGilliss', we again started on our way east, and hoping to meet my husband on the trail very soon.

Before we left Fort Walsh Joe said, "How much money you got?" I answered laughingly, "Only Five Dollars."

"Well, we can't go far on that," he exclaimed. Of course Joe had his gun, and like all pioneers of his day, he was a good shot, so we had plenty of game for food. I knew as soon as I met Charlie there would be plenty of money, and anyway, even if we had to go the whole way to Winnipeg, I could get the money my father had bequeathed to me.

But our immediate need was money, right away, and as luck favoured us, I met an old Indian Trader, who knew my father years ago. When he learned of our plight he lent me Twenty Dollars, happy to be of use to us.

Now we continued our journey, by way of Batoche, where my mother's family lived. Liza, now Mrs. George Ness, decided to come along with us and get her inheritance that lay in trust for her in Winnipeg.

She brought her two very small girls with her. We parted company with Mrs. McGilliss, and now my sister with her children, I, with my little ones and Joe Brown set out again. Liza brought her own democrat and two horses.

When we left Batoche, spring was well on the way and the trail was very wet and muddy. Day after day I expected to meet Charlie and wondered what was keeping him so long, and when the wagons sank into the mud traps up to the hubs, and the horses got mired, the children became tired and began to cry, how I longed for Charlie's help and the chance to cast the whole burden onto him!

The streams were swollen with the melting snow and the fords were swift, but in time we arrived at the end of the steel, near Flat Creek, after a slow and difficult journey.

"Look here," said Joe, "you women better get into the train caboose, and go to Winnipeg by rail. I'll bring the horses and democrats."

Glad to change our mode of travel, we were delighted to do as he suggested, and the day being warm we left all the blankets and pillows in the wagons. Little did we know what travelling in a caboose meant.

There were no seats in such a car, so we had to sit on the floor, and would you believe it, that train didn't leave until next morning. What a night that was! Our little ones, cold and hungry, cried all night without ceasing. Five little tired bodies and two distracted, weeping mothers.

There was sleep for none of us. But, Oh, how lucky we were that the styles of 1877 called for shirred, full-length skirts and several of them. There was but one thing to do, spread out skirts on the floor, lay our children upon them and cuddle together for warmth. How hard and cold the floor was that night! And uncomfortable, for we couldn't move, as changing our position only

> dragged the skirts off the children. But morning came at last and the train started its journey to Winnipeg.[19]

IN ANOTHER WRITING SEGMENT, MARIE ROSE EXPLAINS that when she arrived home to the Jughandle after her summer's travels, Charlie was beside himself with fear for his family. He had no way of knowing how long they had been away, or if they would ever return. It was experiences like these that, no doubt, demonstrated the wisdom of Charlie's choice to marry Marie Rose, as she proved herself capable, time and again.

Marie Rose wrote about the fear that she experienced when her mother told her that she would marry Charlie Smith, a man Marie Rose described as "twenty years" her senior. Yet, she also noted that Charlie was "determined to win her through love." In the following excerpt Marie Rose notes that "Charlie never refused me any request," so off she ventured again on her own. She also describes how, as a young mother, she cared for her babies while ensuring that all her other work was done. Testament to the scope of her work, Marie Rose noted, "I scarcely had time to pick up my babies, even to nurse them."[20]

While proud of her own skills and independence, Marie Rose also enjoyed the social aspects of the pioneer life. Isolated by distance, the desire to socialize was a real commitment; one must pack up belongings and anticipate anything. Seeking companionship, Marie Rose insisted that she could undertake a visit to a neighbor's residence by "following the wagon tracks." Concerned for her safety, but recognizing her determination, Charlie gave this trip his blessing. However, in this instance Marie Rose noted that this, in the end, was a "foolish trip [she] went upon alone."

Sometimes it is difficult to convince new arrivals that so much wild life was formerly in evidence and when one claims to have seen acres of ground literally covered with wavies and grey geese, their look of unbelief is far from flattering.

Our first home in Pincher was a long, one room house. At one end I had a hammock, made of two ropes of rawhide, with blankets and pillows placed between the ropes as a bed for my baby. I scarcely had time to pick my babies up, even to nurse them, but would stand beside the high hammock until the baby nursed his fill, then covering my breast and giving the rope a push, I went about my work while the swinging cradle lulled the baby to sleep.

I also used an Indian baby bag to wrap my new born babies in. Three times a day, my baby was unwrapped from his bag, and when he felt the freedom about his legs and arms, how did he stretch! This was his exercising period, and he enjoyed it for perhaps an hour each time.

In the morning, after the daily bath, the baby looked forward to being wrapped up in his bag again and placed in his swinging hammock. I should tell you about the moss I used in my Indian baby bag. I bought it from the Northern Indians, and mother taught me to heat it in a frying pan, so if there were any insects hidden in the moss they would be driven out or killed. So much for my babies! Now I am going to tell you about another foolish trip I went upon alone, except for the three little ones.

After settling on the ranch, so far from neighbors, I grew lonesome for the sight of another woman. One day

I announce to my husband, "Charlie," I said, "I want to go to the head of Mill Creek and visit Mrs. Boone."

There was a crew of men cutting logs at the head of Mill Creek, in the foothills of the Rocky Mountains, and Baptiste Boone and his wife were a part of this crew. I knew Mrs. Boone would welcome me and looked forward to a day of pleasure.

"Sure, Mary," he answered, "but you don't know the road."

"I'll just follow the wagon tracks," I replied, for I was determined to go. "Give me a gentle team and I'll be alright."

Charlie never refused me any request, so I prepared for my wild trip, packing a lunch for the children and heading westward.

The trail was very plain to follow when I started cut, but soon grew quite dim. To be sure I was on the right trail, I stopped the team again and again, tied them to a tree and hunted about to see if there were any clearer tracks. This continued until late afternoon and still I saw no sign of another human being, and fear that I had lost my way, took hold of me, for my trail now led through fallen timber.

I tried to hurry the horses, for night was beginning to overtake me and it was becoming cold. I had no wraps for the children, save a blanket and pillow for the baby. By now my way led up one steep hill and down another—as we went further into the foothills—until at last we reached one very steep slope which I was afraid to descend.

I was really scared by this time; I was afraid to go forward, still I was afraid to go back. That hill in front of us was like the sides of a teepee, and I dared not risk the lives of my babies. Darkness kept creeping on. I must hurry!

Taking the children out of the wagon, I set them upon the hill top and alone guided the horses down that awful incline, not for a moment daring to think what would happen those children up there if I failed to reach the bottom, right side up. But heaven was with me! At the bottom I tied the horses to a tree and scrambled up by the hill again. Taking my baby in my arms, and encouraging my five- and seven-year-old boys to follow closely, we slid and rolled to the base.

Now I really was in a dilemma! There were no tracks out of that place, only a single horse trail. But this was not the time to sit and wail. I unhitched the team, and led them a little distance away and again tied them to a tree. I lifted the children back into the wagon, gave them sandwiches and doughnuts and warned them not to move or fight while I was gone.

Down the single trail I ran and ran! Then in front of me loomed another hill which I must climb. At the top I again found a dim trail. It was getting darker and darker; I was running farther and farther away from my babies along the trail.

Fear lent wings to my flying feet as through brush and twigs and swamp I ran. The mud sucked off one of my slippers, but I dare not take time to stop for it. To encourage myself I repeated over and over, "It can't be far now, it can't be." But I was lost, and knew not in which direction was the Mill Camp nor where I had left the children; still I ran on.

At last, breathless, flushed, and crying, I stumbled into camp, with breath enough only to gasp, "The children; the team," and pointing back along the trail I had just come over. Then flinging myself into the friendly arms of Mrs. Boone, I sobbed my hysteria away.

Mr. Boone was at supper, but he left at once, and saddling his horse started off in the direction from which I had come. He was not long in returning, bringing with him the team, and when I had my little family about me, once again, gathered tightly in my arms, an awful picture rose up before my thoughts, of what might have been, for Mr. Boone had found tracks of a bear around that wagon![21]

Having returned safely home, and despite Marie Rose's growing independence, she wrote that Charlie was "boss." Indeed, as historian Lucy Eldersveld Murphy writes "Europeans brought different ideas about marriage with them to the Americas. Roman Catholic priests taught that women should be subordinate to men, especially wives to their husbands." While Murphy goes on to write that "Native people tended to resist the patriarchal European ideas."[22] Marie Rose's writings suggests that she did not feel she could resist, but rather felt no option but to adopt the teachings of the Roman Catholic priests. Given her age and the circumstances of their marriage, Marie Rose knew that she had little recourse in openly challenging Charlie. However, that does not suggest that she was completely dependent on him or complacent with his choices.

Marie Rose felt as though, at times, she had few options, particularly with her frustration with the many times that the "whole gang would crowd around" at the ranch as she tried to tend to her children. Even resorting to emptying the barrels of liquor and replacing it with water did nothing to rid herself of the constant visitors that, at times, even prevented her from providing the care she wanted for her children.

CHARLIE BOSS

The only time I could properly feed my children was when all were asleep. I then prepared a big meal, fed them and let them sleep, too.

Many, many nights, I sat on the end of my long cot, with the children lying crosswise of the bed, packed together like little sardines, watching for fear the boys might upset the lamps and burn my little ones to death, or in their stupidity wander to the bed and fall upon it and crush one that might be sleeping.

One day I planned to get rid of the whole gang for good and children and I would be free of all this nonsense. I emptied the barrels, hiding the liquor and replacing it with water, mustard, red pepper and purgative salts. Now do you think that made them sick? No, siree, they drank it all and never knew the difference.

You will wonder why I did not object to having the house full all the time. I did! And many a time I got really angry, but it was no use, Charlie was boss.

I recall one year, when, as Christmas drew near, Charlie said, "I'll go to the Traders and get some 'plain grub' for the holidays, no fancy stuff this time," and he left. Two days elapsed and Charlie didn't come home. We became anxious and started out to look for him, Cooky[23] and I.

It was a large area to seek over, between home and the store, but by and by Cooky found something unusual looking packed tightly in an old animal den.

It was Charlie! He was still fast asleep in the wagon, which had dropped down into the enlarged cave, and he was still holding one line, but the horses were gone.

Waking up Charlie began to sing, "Raspberry Yam, well am I Smith? I lost two horses. If I am not Smith then I got a wagon, and—eh, look," pointing to the stuff under him. "What do you think of my Christmas pudding?"

It was a mess of broken boxes and torn packages, in which raisin and fruit; flour, biscuits and broken eggs were mixed; not to mention Irish twist and snouse [*sic*; snuff]; the whole thing flavored with coal oil and Jamaica Ginger.[24]

ALONG WITH HER RECOLLECTION OF EVENTS ON the Jughandle Ranch, Marie Rose sought to record historical events. When she was a young married woman, she learned about the treaty negotiations with First Nations on the Plains. She had trade relationships with many of these people via her roles as "Buckskin Mary" and the matriarch of Jughandle Ranch. In addition to this work, Marie Rose relied on her childhood education from the convent to record these events of the transitioning Prairie West, as she witnessed them. In some of her writing, Marie Rose takes the liberty of assuming the voice of the historian. This is where the lines between history and historical fiction become blurry. For the most part, in her longer manuscripts, Marie Rose clearly seeks to record history as she observed it. In her shorter pieces, though, she inserts dialogue and goes beyond the boundaries of that which we might view as fictional.

At some point in the excerpt below, Marie Rose assumes the voice of "the late Colonel MacLeod, C. M. G., the

Commandant of the North West Mounted Police," to relate the treaty terms, particularly at "Blackfeet Crossing on the Bow River on September 17th, 1877." She also assumes the voices of First Nations treaty signatories, and particularly Chief Crowfoot, who she notes said, "The Plains are large and wide, we are the children of the Plains. I hope you look upon the Blackfeet, Bloods, Sarcees as your children and that you will be charitable to them . . . they are wonderful people They never look for riches as long as they have something to eat and wear, they are satisfied."[25] The treaty signed in 1876 was Treaty 6, negotiated and signed at Fort Carlton and Duck Lake with the Cree and Stoney Nakoda First Nations. Today the Crossing that Marie Rose refers to and which she clearly recognized as an important historical location, has been recognized as a Canadian National Heritage Site.

With the amount of detail that Marie Rose includes, it is reasonable to assume that she learned some of these details from her own community of Métis connections, but perhaps also directly from Colonel MacLeod, who was her neighbour.

BLACKFOOT TREATY[26]

This important treaty (of 1876) was brought to a successful close, the several tribes interested being allotted suitable reservations. Following upon this in the same year, came the treaties made at Fort Carlton and Pitt by which was a vast area of territory lying between the Saskatchewan [River] and the Rocky Mountains was taken over by the government. This part of the Northwest was the home of the Cree Nation and was partly populated by the Assiniboines. Both these tribes were at the time in a state of great unrest. When they saw the railway surveying parties and others engaged in the construction of telegraph lines led them to think that an attempt was to be made to drive them from their land and their free life. However they were persuaded of the good intentions of the government towards them and the negotiations had a successful issue. Last and by no means the least in the series came the Blackfeet Treaty.[27] The need for making this treaty had become urgent. The conclusion in 1876 of the treaty with the Crees, Assiniboines and Salteaux Indians being the sixth of the series of treaties up to that time negotiated with the Indians of the Northwest, left but a small portion of the territory lying between the boundary line north of the river and west of the Cypress Hills. This portion of the Northwest was occupied by the Blackfeet, Bloods, Sarcees and Peigan Indians. Some of the most warlike[28] and intelligent tribes of the Northwest. These tribes had for years past been anxiously expecting to be dealt with and had been much disappointed at the delay of the treaty. It was reported to the governor that there was a consensus of opinion among the missionaries settled in that territory and others who were acquainted with the Indians as to the desirability of having such a treaty made at the earliest possible date with a view to preserving the present friendly disposition of the tribes. If they should delay the treaty, the Indians would become hostile. They were easily offended, that's their nature. Having these facts in view and the increasing numbers of white settlers into that part of the country, the late Colonel Macleod, C. M. G., the Commandant of the North West Mounted Police at Macleod had had a great deal with the Blackfeet and had won their confidence and good will to a remarkable degree, so they decided to hold a parley at the Blackfeet crossing on the Bow River on September 17th, 1877, which lasted five days. Some of the younger Indians did not quite understand the meaning of the treaty. The governor made clear to them the intention of the government. He called a big meeting. All the chiefs to the Blackfeet, Bloods, Peigans, Assiniboines and Sarcee Tribes, these forming a semi circle of about one mile, and about four thousand men, woman and children watching the proceedings with the keenest interest, some wondering, what's coming next. The Great Spirit "Ki-shay-manito" has made all things, the sun, the moon, the stars, the Earth, the forests, the swift running waters, it is by the Great Spirit that the Queen "The White Mother" rules over this great country and other countries. The Great Spirit has made the white men and the red men brothers, we should take each other by the hand. Our Great Mother, the Queen loves all her children, white men and red men alike. She wishes to do them all good in this world. The bad white man and the bad red man, she alone does not love them, she will punish them for their wickedness. The good Indian had nothing to be afraid of from the Queen or her officers. You Indians know this to be true. When the bad white men brought you whiskey, quarreled among yourselves, robbed you and made you poor through whiskey, she sent the police to put an end to it. You know how they stopped this and how much good this has done. I have to tell you how pleased the Queen is that you have taken the police by the hand and helped them, obeyed her laws since their arrival. She hopes you will continue to do so. You will always find the police on your side if you keep the Queen's law. The Great Mother heard that the buffalo were being killed very fast. To prevent them from being destroyed, her councillors have made a law to protect them. You understand this law is for your own good. It says that the calves are not to be killed in winter or spring, expecting by the Indians when they are in need of them as food. The cows are not to be killed winter or spring so they can increase. This will save the buffalo and provide you with food for many years to come. Our Great Mother wishes you well. Many years ago our Great Mother made a treaty with the Indians far away by the great waters in the East. A few years ago, again she made a treaty with those beyond the Touchwood Hills and Wood Mountains. Another year a treaty was made with the Crees along the Saskatchewan and now our Mother has sent Colonel Macleod and the councillors to ask you to make a treaty. In a very few years the buffalo will probably be all gone and destroyed, and for this reason our Great Mother wishes to help you to live in the future in some other way. She wishes you to allow her, your white brothers to come and live on your land, to raise cattle and farm the land. Should you agree to this, she will assist you to raise cattle and grain like the white people. Giving you the means of living when the buffalo are no more. She will also pay you and your children, money every year, which you can spend as you like. By being paid in money you cannot be cheated, with that money you can buy what you may need. Our Mother, the Queen wishes us to offer you the same as was accepted by the Crees. I don't mean exactly as your lands are more adapted to raise cattle and cattle would be better for you. The Commissioner will give you your choice whether it will be cattle or farm implements. I already told you I will give you money, I will now tell you how much if you sign the treaty. Every man, woman and child will get twelve dollars each. The money will be paid to the head of each family, himself, his woman and children will get five dollars each every year forever. The chiefs will be paid a larger sum; the chiefs will get a suit of clothes, a medal and a flag, and every three years will get another suit. A reserve of land will be set apart for your-selves and your cattle and upon which no others will be permitted to do anything but yourselves. You can cut trees, brush for firewood and other purposes. No white men or half breeds will be permitted to cut the timber or build on your reserves, if required, roads will be cut through them. Cattle will be given to you and potatoes, the same as are growing at Fort Macleod. The Commissioners would strongly advise the Indians to take cattle, as you understand cattle better than you will farming, for a while. As long as you continue roaming around, about in lodges, ammunition will be issued to you each year and as soon as you sign the treaty, the money will be distributed among you. As soon as you settle down, teachers will be sent to you to instruct your children so they can read books like white children, which is impossible so long as you continue to move place to place. Now I have told you and explained the terms of the treaty which you are asked to sign.

The chiefs came forward, one young man filled the medicine pipe, and presented to the chiefs the biggest (Nina). It's a long stem red stone pipe and the young buck lights it, the chief then takes a few puffs and hold it towards the sun, meaning a great luck and saying a few words in their lingo. Then he passes the pipe to the head Commissioner, then they passed the pipe to the rest of the chiefs. This means a great honor among the Indians. They do not use that decorated pipe only on especial occasions. After which the Indians conversed among themselves before signing the treaty. It was hard for them to give up the Plains and the free life. The chief after talking to his people, turned around to the Commissioner to explain on behalf of his tribe his idea. The Great Spirit (Manito) not the Mother Queen gave us this land. She sent Stamixotokon (Colonel Macleod) and the police to put an end to the traffic in firewater. I can now sleep safely. Before the arrival of the police, when I laid my head down at night, little sound frightened me but now I can sleep sound and not afraid of anything. The Great Mother sent you to these Plains, we hope she will be good to us for many years. We expect to get plenty, we are selfish but we want to get all that is coming to us for the rest of our lives. The chief then went on with the demands he wished to make on behalf of his people. On the last day when the terms of the treaty were accepted, Chief Crowfoot delivered a talk also. I have to speak for my people who are numerous and who rely upon me to follow that offer which, in the future, will be for their good. The Plains are large and wide, we are the children of the Plains. It is our home and the buffalo has been our food always. I hope you look upon the Blackfeet, Bloods, Sarcees as your children and that you will be charitable to them. They all expect me to speak for them and I trust (Ma-ni-to) the Great Spirit will put into their hearts to be good people and into their mind of the men, women and children

> and their future generation. The advice given me and my people has proved to be very good. If the police had not come to these Plains, where would we all be now, bad men and whiskey were killing us so fast that very few of us would have been left today. The police have protected us. I wish them all good trust and that all our hearts will increase in goodness from this time. I am satisfied, I will sign the treaty. This is the condition as long as the sun, the moon, the stars shine, running water in the streams, the Indians get what is coming to them and promises forever and ever. For a long time the Indians could not get used to civilization, they were so accustomed to roaming and living in teepees. They did not like living in houses as they like the open air. It was their nature. You never see an Indian with false teeth nor any with corns on their feet, they are well preserved. They are a wonderful people. They never look for riches as long as they have something to eat and wear, they are satisfied.
>
> Charley Smith, the trader, and many others followed the treaty from place to place. When he finished following the treaty he went to Montana.[29]

While much of Marie Rose's writing is undated, we know that she wrote this piece in 1879. Marie Rose and Charlie did as many other robe and whiskey traders: they "followed the treaties," and, in doing so, they gathered enough money to travel to Montana, gather a herd of cattle and drive them back to their new homestead in the Pincher Creek area of southern Alberta.

Below, Marie Rose no longer demonstrates the fear that she had as a young bride. Rather, she wrote about living this "wonderful life . . . the real life." It was a time of plentiful bounty as they crossed back into Canada from their winter home in Montana, as "game was plentiful, swarms of wild fowls were moving and the lakes and ponds were black with feathered game" and that "The North West Territories was a sportsman's paradise." Indicative of the changing times, Marie Rose wrote that "it is difficult to convince recent arrivals that so much wild life was formerly so plentiful . . . the look of unbelief is far from flattering to the oldtimers."[30]

By this point she spoke with admiration of Charlie, noting that "he had travelled all over the plains and he could tell us of some interesting adventures."

CHARLIE STORIES

That was in the year 1879, and bought a herd of cattle with the treaty money. We wintered in Missoula, Montana, a very pretty valley all settled and a very nice town surrounded with mountains, there was very little open range. You could see nice farms with stock and the farmers looked prosperous. We rented a furnished house and Charley went around those farms during the winter and bought cattle, fine stock, the pick of the country. He had all winter to bargain with the farmers and arranged with them to keep and winter them till spring. He paid a sum on them to hold the deal, clever work. People were very friendly and we had a good time all winter, a wonderful life. In the spring Charley and his man went around from ranch to ranch and gathered the stock he bought. Then we came across into Canada. It was slow travelling, cows calfing on the road but it gave us milk. With the fresh milk and all kinds of wild fowls, what more could any one wish. It was real life. Game was plentiful, swarms of wild fowls were moving and the lakes and ponds were black with feathered game. The beating of those wings, when settling or arising from the water sounded like distant thunder. There were swans, grey geese, wavies,[31] pelicans, ducks and sandhill cranes in untold numbers. Prairie chickens too were plentiful and coveys of this grand game bird were everywhere. The North West Territories was a sportsman's paradise. It is difficult to convince recent arrivals that so much wild life was formerly so plentiful and when one claims to have seen acres of ground literally covered with wavies and grey geese, the look of unbelief is far from flattering to the oldtimers.

After travelling all day, we would be glad to camp and enjoy the camp fire. While we would be resting, enjoying our tea and meal we would listen to some real stories told by Charley Smith. Before we had ever met Charley, he had travelled all over these Plains and he could tell us some interesting adventures. He related that in 1875 buffaloes were so plentiful that they would come quite close around the camp and it was no trouble to get meat. If they killed one, they always picked the best for good steaks and in those days the tongue was a delicacy. In one place there were so many buffalo, we were held up for nearly an hour by a herd in solid formation. After such a herd passed, you would see the dust in the air like clouds. As a rule these buffaloes were not dangerous, only the young cows with calf. They are so big they look clumsy but it takes a good horse to keep up with them when they are running.

> It takes a swift horse to catch them. Horses are sure-footed but these animals have a guarding instinct, quickness of mind and nimbleness of muscle that enables them to keep out of gopher holes. To step into a gopher hole when going at full speed is serious. It means broken limbs. But everyone took a chance in those days. There were no fences, no bridges, no settlers of any kind and this was a free country. During the warm seasons of the year, the rivers and streams were high, swift and dangerous but we made the best of it and crossed them. When we came to high river or stream, there was no trouble and it seemed quite natural for us to unload our belongings and get to work to make a raft or boat out of parchment skins and a few long poles using raw-hide for ropes. They would load that boat and tie it at the end of the horse's tail, a good swimming horse, and a good strong man, a swimmer, would ride the horse and cross and re-cross until all our belongings, carts, women and children were safe on the opposite bank. It was a hard task but we succeeded and there was never an accident. Poor oldtimers, they saw a lot of hardships on these Plains, nevertheless they lived through good and bad times. Always happy and they had strength and willingness. They were not looking for riches just to live and be happy.[32]

Indeed, Marie Rose relished hearing the stories of adventurers, like those of her husband Charlie and others. This included her neighbour, Lionel Brooke who established the Chinook Ranch. Brooke was a remittance man, a class of British who were sent to the new country with money, more as a way for their families to rid themselves of their poor potential rather than believing that they would actually succeed in the Prairie West. In Brooke's case, he was born "in the midst of immense wealth set in Victorian England." He was reliant on quarterly stipends from his family, which allowed him to establish the Chinook Ranch, not far from the Jughandle Ranch. According to local historian Farley Wuth, Brooke was no better a rancher than businessman. It was often the case that Brooke went from plenty to little, depending on the support from home. Brooke travelled with Indigenous Peoples, and reportedly spent some of his stipends on buying horses and equipment for them. Joining them often on hunting trips, the Bearspaw Nakoda First Nation reportedly gave Brooke the name "Chief Window Pane," due to his "distinctive look with that monocle."[33]

Regardless of their standing in the home country, these remittance men were welcomed by their new neighbours who, like Marie Rose, were happy to learn about the new sport of polo and to hear about their worldly travels. They contributed an air of social class to events, particularly Lionel Brooke, who was said to have an air of aristocracy. Perhaps it was a pleasure for Marie Rose to allow her imagination to explore these "different countries and places such as South Africa, Italy, Norway, Bermuda, West Indies, Iceland, California, Japan, China, Honolulu . . . Just imagine the amount of money it would take for these trips." Yet, in the end, Lionel Brooke chose to spend his retirement in Marie Rose's own boarding house in Pincher Creek. As she notes, clearly impressed, after all of the first class worldly travel, "to think that he would choose Pincher Creek for a retiring life."[34]

LIONEL BROOKE

One of the oldtimers in the summer of 1885, the year of the Rebellion, a Mr. Godsal sold the Butte Ranch to Mr. Lion Brookes who, with Mr. Hatfield, went into ranching. They were partners for a few years but were very different in disposition. Mr. Hatfield was quiet and very reserved while Lion Brookes was a live wire and liked a good time with the young people. After a few years they dissolved partnership and Mr. Brookes moved to the Chinook Ranch in the Beauvais Lake District and there he ran a horse ranch with Mr. and Mrs. Brown in charge. Mrs. Brown was an English woman, full of pep, a good cook, very kind and nice to everybody. Lion Brookes' money was not object to him, many thousands of dollars he spent on that place. He was very free, sending money to everybody and helping the poor. In later years he followed the wild life, he would go into the mountains travelling with the Stonies,[35] living with them and many times had to put up with [the women's] cooking. You can imagine a lot and then some but it was a change from civilization. Among them he was a big man (Nina), living in a teepee, travelling with pack horses and travois along the mountain living on wild game, lots of fish and wild berries. He liked the Stoney Indians' life, they were honest with him and he was a chief among them they called him "white man with big glass eyes." He often says that he would much rather be with the Stony Indians than with white people. Lion Brookes helped the poor and many others and he spent lots of money since he came to this country. He has taken trips to different countries and places such as; South Africa, Italy, Norway, Bermuda,

West Indies, Iceland, California, Japan, China, Honolulu, and many places in British Columbia, Saskatchewan and Alberta. Just imagine the amount of money it would take for these trips, travelling first class. The places he has seen and the good times and to think that he would choose Pincher Creek for a retiring life. At one time he lived in a shack at the head of Pincher Creek, a few miles further than where Riviere lives, better known as (Frenchy) Husky Ranch. He can tell you many thrilling adventures of his travels. In some ways he is rather queer. One thing he does not care for, women or children. He often says that you can train a dog better than you can train children. Well, that's his idea. When the Boer War was on, he paid his own way over and before it was over he was taken prisoner by the Boers. He is a man always looking for excitement, that's his ambition. For eats, he prefers bacon, hard tack and strong black tea. When on the Chinook Ranch, he had a Mr. and Mrs. Brown working for him. It was a lively place and people would gather there to have fun, bucking horses, roping, &c. Some would go there for a good square meal, all at L. Brookes' expense. He never refused anyone any help. Real old days of oldtimers, nothing but excitement and lots of Jamaica ginger to drink. Once in awhile some one would have a permit for the real Mckay.[36] Mr. and Mrs. John Brown made enough money from Brookes to build a nice ranch near the Chinook Ranch and later they moved to their own place and lived happily. In a few years they sold to kettles and returned to England. While they were ranching, John Brown sent to England for two of his nieces, both nice looking girls. They were good riders and you always saw them riding around

> the country with their Uncle John. Their name was "Easton."[37] In those days everything looked bright and prosperous. Wherever you went, you saw riders looking for mavericks in a bunch of cattle. Some of the readers may not understanding the meaning of "maverick." It means calves without any brand. The law was not very severe those days rustling a maverick was a joke. Wherever you looked on the prairies you would see cattle grazing, no fences to bother with, they would roam around like buffalo. The country looked rich, but that's a thing of the past. Mr. L. Brookes still remains in Pincher Creek is quite smart and has his occasional little spree. Although he was crippled by being thrown off a horse, he still likes the wild life and it cannot be too wild for him.[38]

As she related stories of her neighbours, such as Lionel Brooke, Marie Rose interjected to share her perspective on her married life. On one of their trips, Marie Rose and Charlie stopped in at a local store, where she was proud to trade some of her leather work for groceries for her family. Encountering some difficulties on the return trip home, Marie Rose and Charlie had to make camp for the night, arriving home the next day to friends who "had a bottle of scotch which certainly cheer Charley." As Marie Rose wrote, she "did not like my husband drinking but I had to put up with it . . . in those days men were boss and women had to obey."[39] Demonstrating an ability for philosophical thought, Marie Rose noted that "My married life was full of trials and tribulations and whether it is worth the price you have to pay for it depends altogether upon how much love is between each other and how gallantly we can play the game."[40]

MEN BOSS

They returned and Mr. Boone told me there was a bear in that locality. I would never have forgiven myself if anything had happened to my children. I often thought how foolish it was of me to venture into the mountains not knowing where I was going. The young and foolish do not know danger. I had come to visit for only a day but there came a snow storm and I had to remain there for two weeks. When the weather cleared up, Mr. Boone brought us home. We had a good road, I was altogether on the wrong road, however I made it although I had a tough trip. My husband was certainly glad to see me home, safe with children. But when I told him about my trip, he said he would never let me go away again, you foolish woman.

On the Old Man River[41] a man named Gillingham opened a store. I think he was part Jew and was married to a Japanese. One lovely morning in September, it was just like summer, I suggested to my husband that we go to Gillingham's. We drove there and I showed Gillingham some buskin gloves that I had brought along and told him I wanted to trade them for groceries. He was quite pleased with the gloves. They gave us a nice hot dinner and it was the first time we had ever seen a [Japanese] woman. She was dressed in silk, a very good cook and very pleasant. After dinner we traded, I had three dozen pairs of gloves (buckskin) so I had quite a lot groceries. People those days were kind to each other. They fed our team and would not charge us, asked us to call again. When our business was completed, we started for home. I was pleased with my trade. When about half way it commenced to rain a little and it turned very cold. Without warning the north wind began to blow and snow. Then came the blizzard, we could not see our horses and we had missed the road. It was so bad Charley wanted to return to Gillingham's. I objected as we were nearer home, but it grew darker and stormier, very cold for the driver. It was so warm when we left in the morning that we were not prepared for such a storm, we had no warm coats with us. I asked Charley if there were not some coulees around and if we might not drive into one and upset, so let us unhitch the team, crawl under the democrat until morning. We had a canvas for the groceries and we had a badger robe and a homemade quilt and as soon as the break of day came and we could see good enough to travel we started for home. We never put in such a cold night, we were glad to get home and have a nice hot cup of coffee. Wallace Nicoll and McMillan who had stayed at our house all night, and stayed up most of the night waiting for us, were there to greet and they had a bottle of scotch which certainly cheered Charley. That was just the start of a good spree, they then sent one of the boys for a supply and they kept this up for a week. In those days men were boss and women had to obey, right or wrong. I obeyed to keep peace in the family. I did not like my husband drinking but I had to put up with it. Of course when my husband had his friends with him, they had their own living quarters but I did the cooking and the work. All the oldtimers gathered at the Jug Handle Ranch and they would have a good time among themselves. That was all the amusement in the country at that time. Drink and be merry for tomorrow you may die. They would sit around and tell yarns, sing songs and pass around the drinks. Charley had as many as fifteen one time and they had a whale of a time. They called them Peter McLaren's mill gang.[42] Sometimes it was laughable and again I would be very tired of them. My married life was full of trials and tribulations and whether it is worth the price you have to pay for it depends altogether upon how much love is between each other and how gallantly we can play the game.

Often in these jamborees George J. Brown (Kootenay Brown) would mix with them, then they would have lots of fun. As I mentioned before Brown was very clever. He would say "Boys, you don't know anything," and they would all laugh at him "Oh Brown, another little drink won't do us any harm" and he would continue: some day in the future you'll see people flying like birds in the air. He also predicted that in those mountains near Kootenay Lakes there would be a summer resort. You know I can see it coming, same as I see this liquor in my glass.[43]

Marie Rose shared the musings of this neighbour, John George Kootenai Brown, who accurately predicted that many would eventually travel from all over the world to this land that Marie Rose so loved. As one of the earliest pioneers on the Prairies, Marie Rose clearly appreciated the freedom to travel for miles on the range without the "impediment of fences … those were the days. When the rancher's wives in cooking their family meals … the early rancher always squatted where he could find a spring and plenty of range."[44] These were the days when the large, sprawling ranches were established, some of those remaining today, such as the Walrond Ranch. In this writing, she recalled memories for her of earlier days when, wherever one looked they would see buffalo grazing, as she noted that "wherever you look on the Prairie you will see cattle roaming."[45] Marie Rose and Charlie "went as cooks on the wagons," no doubt again drawing on skills learned as a member of the Delorme family.

Marie Rose used the term "squatters," which is what settlers called Métis people. The more accurate term is "road allowance communities." As scholar and Métis Elder Maria Campbell notes, road allowances in Western Canada reflected crown land that was set aside for roadways for future development. The dispossession of the Métis from Red River and Batoche after the events of 1869–70 and 1885, as Campbell wrote, "created a diaspora that is the source of the poverty, rootlessness, and loss of identity being experienced by the Métis people today." Dispossessed of their land, many Métis settled along the road allowances, and were thus regarded by governments as "squatters." At the time, road allowance communities "numbered in the hundreds" in Alberta, Saskatchewan and Manitoba.[46] While not acknowledging this, Marie Rose would likely have been aware of these communities.

In the following excerpt, Marie Rose also shared with readers her devotion to her faith and its Roman Catholic leaders. She noted that because of Father Albert Lacombe, her community of Pincher Creek, was "blessed" with a convent. Lacombe was an Oblate missionary who traveled with the Métis brigades and is credited with establishing missions at Lac Ste. Anne and Saint-Paul-des-Cris (and later at St-Paul-de-Métis). The Roman Catholic clergy have a long history with the Métis, eventually influencing them to assume a more sedentary lifestyle. They also influenced their views of marital relationships and the roles of women, often encouraging a patriarchal ideology not common in most Indigenous societies. In their attempts to influence the Métis, Roman Catholic missionaries often relied on Métis women who were "the educators and transmitters of culture in the home and had the most influence on the children or future generations."[47] It is unsurprising, then, that Marie Rose acquiesced to Father Lacombe's suggestion that they send her young daughter Mary Anne to a convent school in Quebec.

FENCES AND FREEDOM

When all the settlers were ranchers and everyone was neighborly and friendly, riding mile after mile no fences to trouble you. Those were the days. When the ranchers' wives in cooking their meals, the cowboys would drop in at meal times to get a square. The early rancher always squatted where he could find a spring and plenty of range with good hay land. They would put up shacks and corrals on his holdings and ranged his cattle for miles around. About in November before the cold weather would come, the fall roundup commenced, the rancher and his men then rode the range continuously for about two months so as to have his cattle near the place so that when severe weather set in they would be close at hand to feed. Cattle always look for water and generally stay around some open spring.

After the fall frost when the grass begins to get poor, the calves are weaned for four days and four nights. The calves compete with their mothers to see who can make the most noise. Poor animals, they sure bawl for one another. After several days the cows join the main herd but the calves remain in corral to be fed through the winter. About the 1st of April the new calves begin to arrive, from then until the end of June. The branding starts in the month of August. Wherever you look on the prairie you will see cattle roaming around with different brands. Prices for cattle were very high; we sold good milch cows[48] for a hundred and twenty-five dollars, while beef steers demanded an average of sixty dollars. Cattle were always in good shape as grass grew abundantly and luxuriously. In 1892 the different cattle men decided to travel to Strathmore to ship their surplus stock. Each outfit had his own cowboys and mess wagon. Charley and I went as cooks on our wagon. I had a baby girl and she became known as "The Prairie Girl."[49] We all met at a point on the Old Man River where the bridge is east of Cowley, travelling thence to the lower Walrond Ranche,[50] where we camped the first night. Some of riders acted as night herders, while others looked after the herds during the day. Much of the travelling was done in early morning or late afternoon and evening, letting the cattle rest during the heat of the day. Several days elapsed before we reached the shipping point. Finally we got there. After receiving our cheques we sojourned to Calgary to invest our earnings. Generally the cowboys would spend all their earnings, going home broke but happy. Western life.

In 1883 on New Year's morning we started for mother's. An old French custom is to visit your parents New Years and to have breakfast with them. It was a very cold morning and the snow was deep, we had driven over in a sleigh. While there we heard a roaring noise in the mountains, like thunder, then the Chinook arrived with a warm wind, that was a real one. Freinds [*sic*] and relatives were sitting at the table having a good meal, laughing and talking and before we had finished the meal, snow was melting fast, c'est pas croyable,[51] water was all over the flat. The warm wind and hot sun was like summer weather. We did not like to leave the crowd having a good time meeting each other before noon but we were obliged to take our sleigh home and return in democrats. These New Year celebrations lasted until the 8th January, feasting and dancing during the whole week at different houses where everything is prepared for such an event and for a crowd. There is a different class of people today compared to the oldtimers who were so friendly and helped one another. Times have changed and even our Chinook wind is changed and we will never see the country like it used to be. The old pioneer days were happy days and wants were few.

Many years elapsed before we were blessed with a convent. At the dear request of Father Lacombe, the mission of Pincher Creek ever dear to his heart would not be a real mission without the Sisters. Accordingly he invited les Filles des Jesus (Daughters of Jesus) of Three Rivers to come without fear or refusal. In January 1904 the families of Pincher Creek with Reverend Fathers Lacombe and Blanchet warmly welcomed the arrival of the Sisters. There were Reverend Sisters

> St. Guenole, St. Alimene and Oneour. At first their small home permitted them to give private lessons only including religious instruction. But soon, through the generous co-operation of Mr. T. Lebel, Mr. Pelletier and many others, whose generosity will long be graciously remembered, a more spacious building was erected on the hill not far from the church. Mr. T. Hinton being the contractor, the new convent Rermaria[52] soon had fifty boarders under the superiorship of Rev. Mother Angelique and several other Sisters.[53] Father Lacombe's cherished mission, to devote their services to the school and church. The saintly Bishop Legal[54] on the occasion of his visits always congratulated the pupils of the convent for their piety and excellent conduct.[55]

While not mentioned by Marie Rose, some of her children boarded at the convent in Pincher Creek. Marie Rose remained steadfast in her support of the Roman Catholic missionaries, despite losing a young daughter who she had agreed to send to Quebec to be educated by the Roman Catholic nuns.

left: Author (right) and Donald McCargar, great-grandson of Marie Rose Delorme Smith. Donald's jacket was commissioned in honour of the designation of Marie Rose as a person of national historic significance. AUTHOR'S COLLECTION

below: Marie Rose Delorme Smith wearing the medals of her two sons who died serving in Europe during the First World War. Undated. SHIRLEY-MAE/DONALD McCARGAR

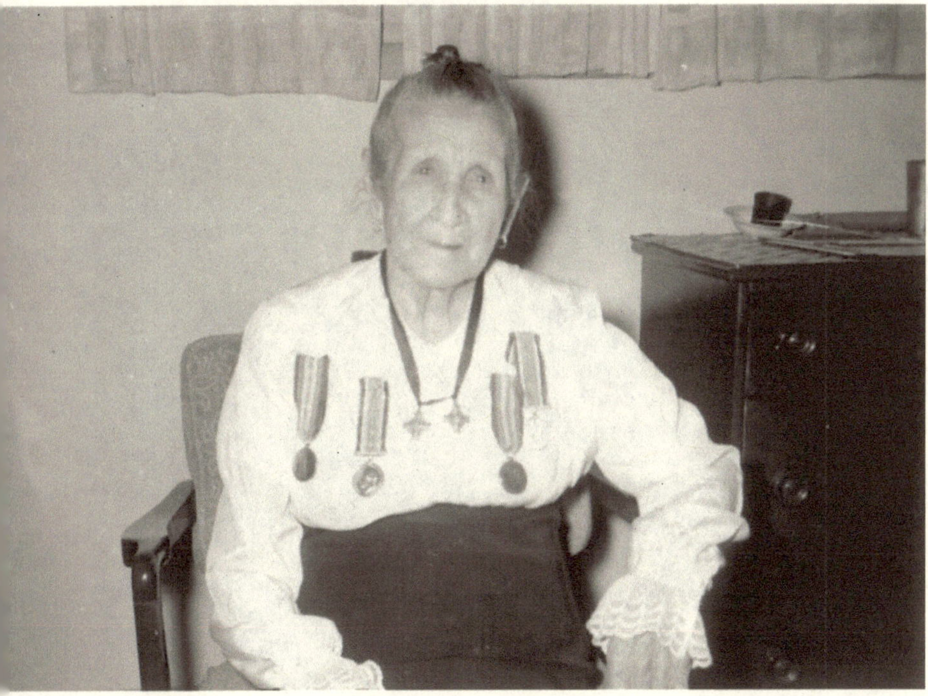

above: Marie Rose playing the accordion, only one of the many musical instruments that she played. Undated. SHIRLEY-MAE/DONALD MCCARGAR

below: Marie Rose stands in the centre of the front row. To the right of her are John George "Kootenai" Brown and Charlie Smith. Undated. SHIRLEY-MAE/DONALD MCCARGAR

Marie Rose with her mother (left), daughter (standing at the back), and grandchildren. Undated. SHIRLEY-MAE/DONALD McCARGAR

Marie Rose and child. Undated. SHIRLEY-MAE/DONALD McCARGAR

Marie Rose with a baby and older daughter Mary Anne, who later passed away at the convent in Quebec. Undated. SHIRLEY-MAE/DONALD McCARGAR

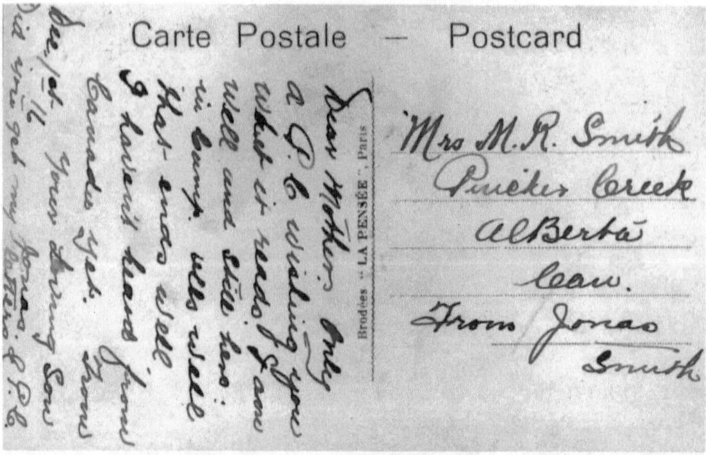

above: Postcard to Marie Rose from her son Private Jonas Smith while he was serving in Europe during the First World War. December 1916. SHIRLEY-MAE/ DONALD McCARGAR

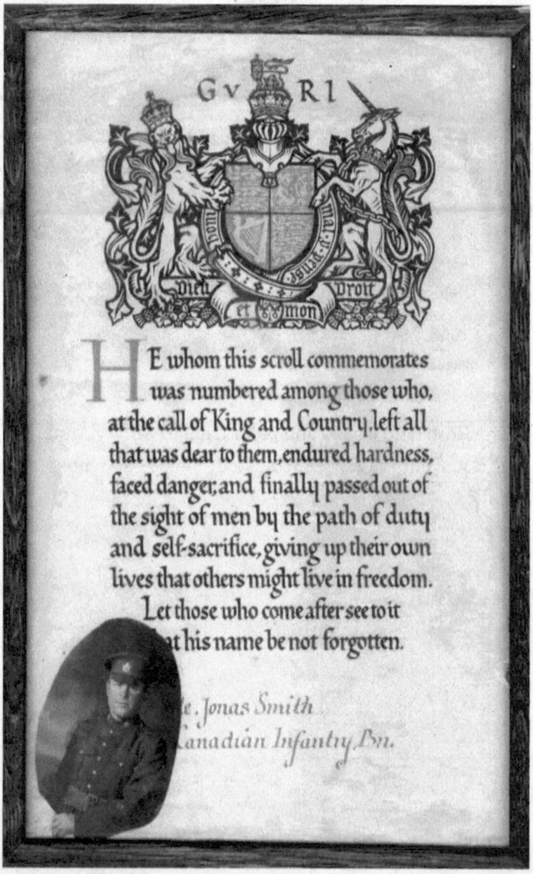

right: Memorial card for Private Jonas Smith, killed in action on August 15, 1917 in France. SHIRLEY-MAE/ DONALD McCARGAR

right: Marie Rose, with her daughter Madeleine Eva walking on the streets of Edmonton. Undated. SHIRLEY-MAE/DONALD McCARGAR

below: Models believed by family members to be wearing traditional clothing made by Marie Rose. Undated. SHIRLEY-MAE/DONALD McCARGAR

top left: Author with Jock Carpenter (right), Marie Rose's granddaughter and author of *Fifty Dollar Bride*. Undated.

AUTHOR'S COLLECTION

bottom left: Author with Shirley-Mae McCargar (seated) and Doug McCargar (left). Undated.

AUTHOR'S COLLECTION

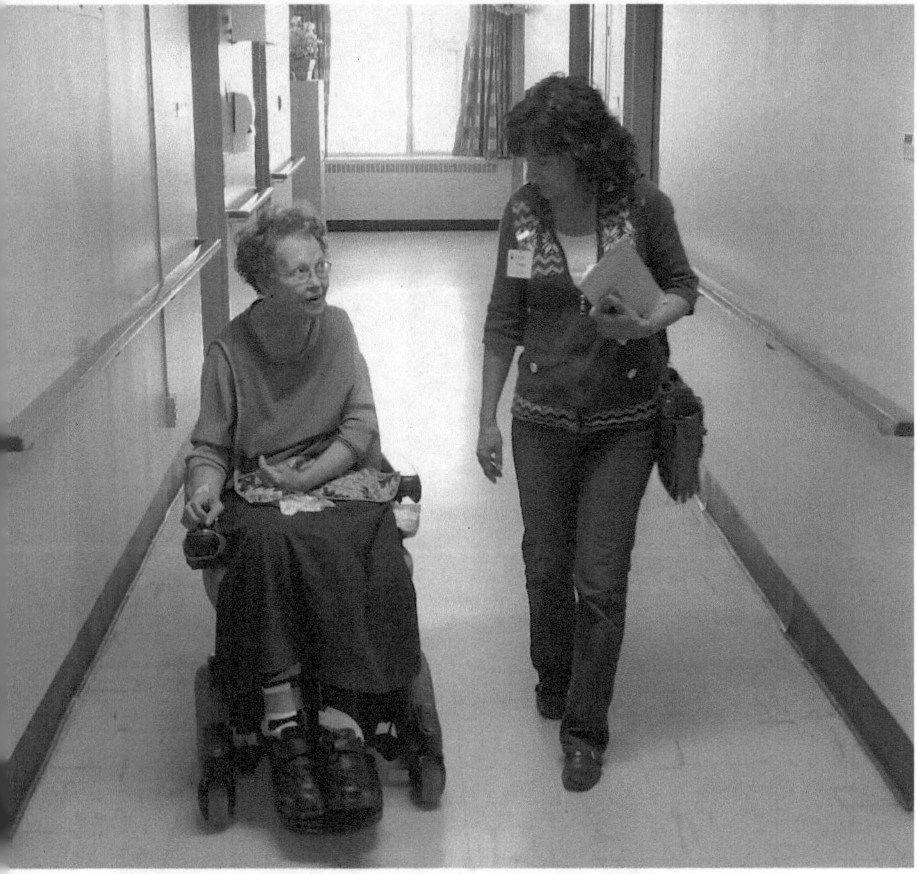

Author with Shirley-Mae McCargar at the start of the research while establishing the relationship with the extended family network. Undated. AUTHOR'S COLLECTION

left: The plaque commemoraring establishment of the St. Albert Mission, where Marie Rose travelled to marry Charlie Smith. Undated. AUTHOR'S COLLECTION

below: Headstone of Charlie Smith's gravesite, Pincher Creek, Alberta. Undated. AUTHOR'S COLLECTION

Donald McCargar, Marie Rose's great-grandson, wearing traditional clothing made by her. Undated. SHIRLEY-MAE/DONALD MCCARGAR

above: Family burial ground, at Pincher Creek, including the plaque commemorating Marie Rose's life. Undated. AUTHOR'S COLLECTION

below: Plaque about Marie Rose that was included in a museum collection from Library and Archives Canada, entitled "Hidden in Plain Site." Undated. AUTHOR'S COLLECTION

Author (second from left) with members of Marie Rose Delorme Smith's family. Undated. AUTHOR'S COLLECTION

above: Kermaria Convent, Pincher Creek, for which Marie Rose worked to raise funds and where some of her children attended school. Undated.
PEEL'S PRAIRIE PROVINCES ARCHIVES

opposite: A letter written by Marie Rose to Bishop Taché in French, which she learned to speak and write while at the convent in St. Boniface, Manitoba. September 15, 1893. AUTHOR'S COLLECTION

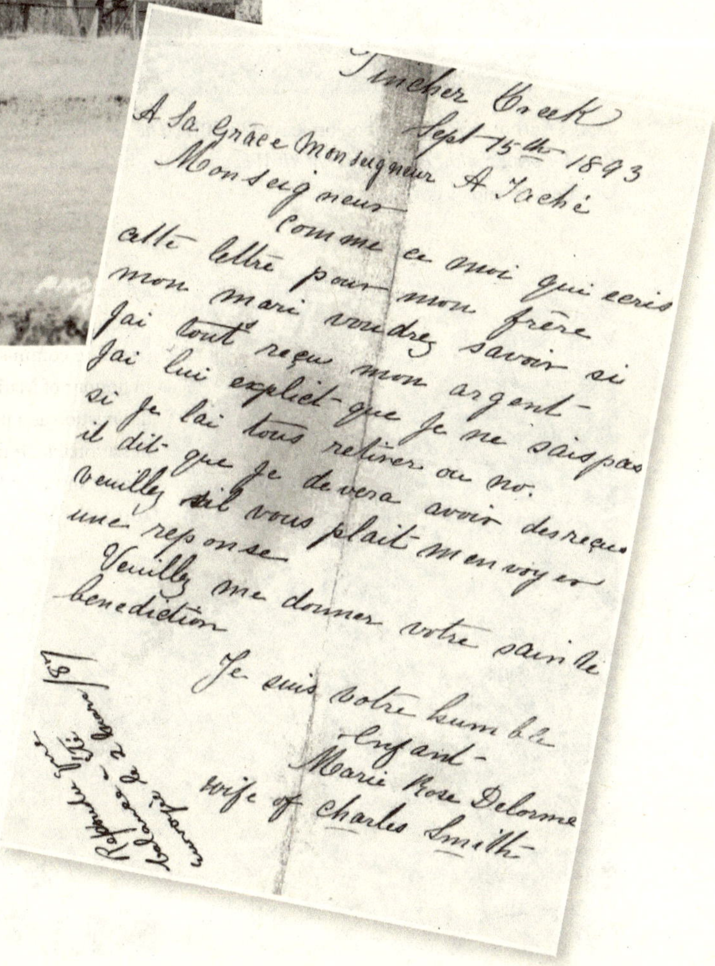

Pincher Creek
Sept 15th 1893

A Sa Grâce Monseigneur A Taché

Monseigneur

Comme ce moi qui ecris cette lettre pour mon frère mon mari voudrez savoir si jai tout reçu mon argent. Jai lui explict que je ne sais pas si je lai tous retirer ou no. il dit que je devera avoir des reçus Veuillez s'il vous plait m'envoyer une reponse

Veuillez me donner votre sainte benediction

Je suis votre humble
Enfant
Marie Rose Delorme
wife of Charles Smith

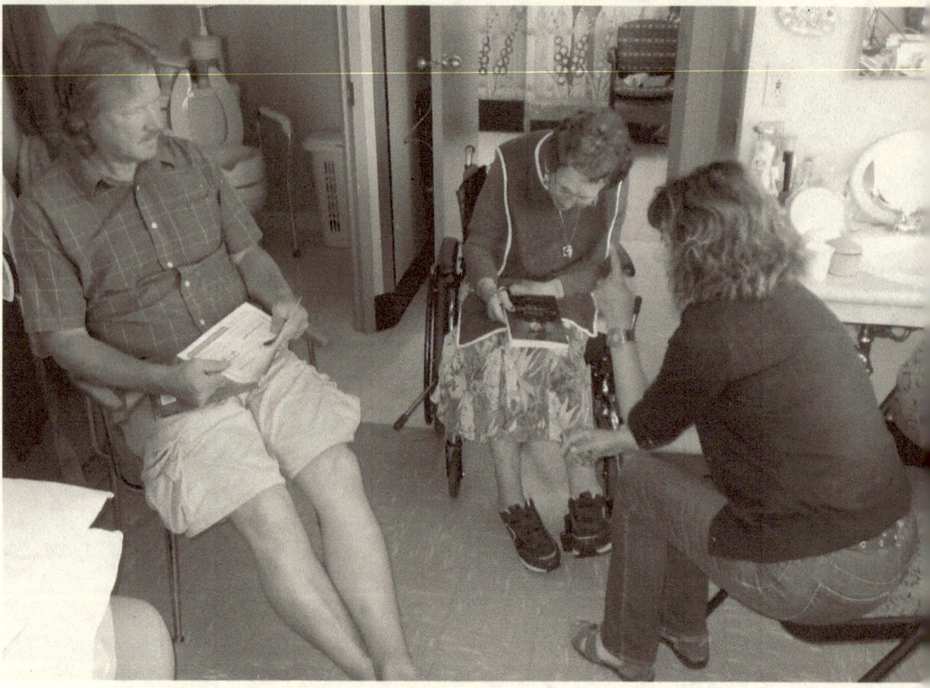

above: Author sharing new book released in 2012, *The Identities of Marie Rose Delorme Smith: Portrait of a Métis Woman,* with Shirley-Mae McCargar. Undated. AUTHOR'S COLLECTION

left and below: Donald McCargar wearing the jacket he commissioned in honour of Marie Rose's designation as a person of national historic significance. Undated. AUTHOR'S COLLECTION

4 — Chronicler of Life Stories

As she sat in her little apartment that first night, eating her first home cooked meal in years, a great wave of contentment came over her. She realized that she had been wise in deciding to carry on regardless of the odds, and to try to make something of a life that to her had looked so useless a few years previously . . . Many times she would find herself comparing her own happy home life with the lives of the people with whom she came in contact, who seemed to have so much more financially than she had had, but who could not boast of being happier or even as happy as she had been in the all too short years that she had spent with her family and their lack of luxuries.[1]

STORYTELLING IS A KEY ASPECT OF MÉTIS culture and community. As scholar Yvonne Poitras Pratt notes, "within each person lies a story that has the power to change their lives and, if shared, the potential to transform the world of others . . . it is the living quality of stories that make them such a potent tool of transformation."[2] Marie Rose confirmed that she often heard stories from her mother, and those stories were clearly shared with her children and grandchildren. For Marie Rose, that she recorded many of her memories and stories demonstrates that they served as a tool of transformation in her own life.

Most of Marie Rose's writing was presented as memoir and historical narrative. She clearly desired to record the stories of the pioneers that formed part of her community in southern Alberta. Readers learned of her connection with legendary Prairie characters such as John George "Kootenai" Brown, the first park warden of Waterton Lakes National Park. Marie Rose wrote of Kootenai's observations that, someday, tourists would come from around the world, drawn by the natural beauty of the Waterton Lakes area. There was an admiration in Marie Rose's writings for world travelers such as Kootenai Brown and "Sir" Lionel Brooke, the British remittance man spoken of earlier, who ranched near the Jughandle and who spent his final years in Marie Rose's boarding house in the town of Pincher Creek.

While some, such as William Rodney, have portrayed Kootenai Brown as a Canadian "Davey Crockett," a rugged Plains hero, Marie Rose, a friend of Kootenai's, noted that he was the "first homesteader in the southern district of the Western Canada Plains," and had "good and bad qualities." Below, Marie Rose shares in greater detail the account of the death of Kootenai's first wife, Olive D'Lonais, a Métis woman who attended the same convent as Marie Rose.

OLIVE'S DEATH

There have been many interesting stories about the great notable man, John George Brown (Kootenay Brown). It is really too bad that we never got a full account of the life of Kootenay Brown before his death. What little we know of him and his adventures are very interesting, As he came into the country like the rest of the oldtimers, he liked the wild life but he was a perfect gentlemen. In 1878 when John George Brown made his trip, it constituted the first journey across the plains of western Canada by pack horses. To get from wild horse creek[3] to the prairies of the west, took Brown around the shores of what is now Waterton Lakes in the south west corner of Alberta. The more than ordinary grandeur of the scenery, the rich abundance of prairie grass, the plains and the blue water made the traveller wish for a home on the shores of the lake. But before he settled, he wandered around to see more country. With his pack ponies he landed in Winnipeg. He passed by Duck Lake and there he met about fifty families, mostly half breeds and quarter breeds.[4] Brown always liked company of any kind and he stayed there some time with them. Brown always had new views in his mind. After a stay in Winnipeg, he crossed to the States and in Fort Benton he married his first wife. Archie Rouleau relates that in the year 1883 he was stationed at the police detachment of the Kootenay River for about two years and he had a man with him. Rouleau was a scout. As the Indians were killing cattle on the Cochrane Stock Ranch, he was sent there to police the country. He patroled the range and glad to get some place to rest, he would stop at Kootenay's Place, Kootenay Lakes, present name Waterton Park. Mr. John George Brown used to tell him about his travels, where he came from and where he got married in Fort Benton, Montana, he said he married a nice quarter breed woman, good looking, educated at the convent in St. Boniface, Winnipeg, Manitoba. Her maiden name was Olive Delany. While in Benton they had two children, both girls. They lived very happy until he got into trouble killing a man, in self defence.

The vigilants were going to lynch and hang him, but he heard about it and some of his friends helped him to get across the border. They gave him a good saddle horse, a pack pony and what he needed. While they were getting ready they told him to go to a certain place near a creek with thick brush to hide and they would meet him. This happened during the night and the vigilantes were on his trail. That's the way he got away (by the skin of his teeth). Then he came to the North West Territories and landed in Kootenay Pass. There he chose a spot between the two lakes, the Upper Lake and Lower Lake. Out of logs cut in the mountains, a house and barn were built. The first homesteader in the southern district of the western Canada plains began ranching but he did mostly hunting. This homestead was taken before anyone thought of surveys and all the improvements were made long before it was filed on. In 1881 he sent for his family and there they lived on wild game and fish, mostly fish. John George Brown was a clever man, well educated, a most daring but dangerous man. He told some very thrilling stories about himself. He had good and bad qualities and a winning way. In 1883 Mrs. J. G. Brown gave birth to a baby boy. The only help she had was a Stony [woman], imagine the care she would get, not very good. She did not regain her usual health after that birth and Brown did not seem to realize how sick she was when she would complain of not feeling well. Between sickness and loneliness, only Indians calling there, she got worse and she had three little ones to take care of. Brown, he'd get on his horse, his daily routine, go away to different detachments and loaf around. It was while he was on one of the trips that the woman died, she only had the hired man to look after her. The poor children did not realize that their mother was dying. Imagine what a sad sight, a cold breathless mother lying dead and the little ones creeping around on her calling, "Mama, sleep no more, wake up." The hired man tried to comfort the little ones. There was no sign of Brown coming and he could not keep her any longer so he found some boards around the place and made a rough box for a coffin. Now to put her in, it was a task. He never could handle her alone, she was so heavy. He laid the box near the bed, tried to roll her into it with her blankets wrapped around her and when she rolled she fell face down. The little ones were screaming and crying telling him to leave their Mama alone, it was heart breaking. Now to take her to the grave, already dug, he tied a rope on the box and jerked it by the aid of his saddle horse out side the door and dragged her to the grave on the brow of the Lower Lake, where she lies.[5] Next day Brown got home. As soon as he threw himself off his horse, the three little ones ran up to him crying and telling him that Mama was gone, pointing towards the hill. He did not quite understand them. When he went into the house, the hired man was cooking. "Well, Mr. Brown, she is gone. I did the best I could and I could not keep her any longer. Her last wish to tell you to be kind to her little ones and to put them in some school." The hired man later told that he never wanted to see such grief. Brown sat down with his little ones around him and sobbed along with them. Shaking his head "Oh, my God forgive me, I did not dream she was so sick. Oh my God, what will I do. I'll never forgive my self, poor Olive." Then he would cry. The next day some Stony Indians arrived. Expecting to be fed, disappointed when Brown told them that his wife was dead and buried. Brown could not rest at all. He got ready and with his three children he went to Fort MacLeod to find Father Lacombe to place his children in some school. Father Lacombe, kind hearted, knew Olive well and said a mass for her soul. John George Brown was a lonely man. Nothing to do but to return home. For the first few weeks, he was sleepless, walked the floor, visit the grave and talk to himself. Many years rolled by, Brown never forgot his grief. Any time he would mention it, you would see tears roll down his cheeks. This happened many years ago still many oldtimers have never forgotten.

Brown was of a wandering disposition, he studied nature and beautiful scenery. He was on his horse a good deal, riding around, hunting was his delight. When he came to Pincher Creek, he had good times with the boys.[6]

Unlike his biographer, William Rodney, who hailed Kootenai Brown a Prairie hero, Marie Rose preferred to record Brown's history as she witnessed it, noting his "wandering ways" that caused problems for his partners. While Marie Rose clearly viewed herself as a chronicler, and her manuscripts are important resources for those seeking to understand the social history of the Métis and of the early settlement of the Prairie West, she was selective in the stories she shared. When she did most of her writing, likely in the mid-twentieth century, Indigenous Peoples did not always enjoy the freedom to openly embrace their identity and history. Yet, Marie Rose desired to record this social history of the Métis. We might view Marie Rose's use of memory in her writing in the way that Indigenous poet Joy Harjo uses it "to retrace the past not as an inducement to curl inwards on oneself, as if it were a point in time without escape route, but rather as a dynamic process to reaffirm ancient heritages and proceed forward on a path of constant renewal."[7] For Marie Rose, her writing—complete with factual omissions, but nonetheless with assertions made about the inner thoughts of those she wrote about—can be viewed as a dynamic process as she assumes the role of an omniscient observer. Her writing can also be seen as an affirmation of her ancestry and of her current role as a matriarch and important community member.

With this in mind, in the excerpt below, Marie Rose relates the story of the "Two Rebellions," noting that she writes based on the recollections of her "brother-in-law, George Ness." Ness served as a Justice of the Peace in Batoche during the 1885 events, so it was unlikely that he supported Louis Riel. Marie Rose concludes that Riel's "grave mistake" was permitting the "shooting of Tom Scott." As she tells it, the act of shooting Scott was not supported by most of Riel's soldiers. While she does not tell readers this, among Riel's soldiers were her uncles, Joseph and Norbert Delorme, both of whom fled the area for southern Alberta and eventually went across the border after the end of the fighting. According to historian Diane Payment, when the leaders of the Métis were dispersed, Norbert Delorme was in the "Battleford area" for a time.[8] Many of the Métis soldiers were mobile, likely living in various areas, and depending on the assistance of family members in other locations, such as Marie Rose's family in the Pincher Creek area.

Given the mobility of some Métis at this particular time, Marie Rose's source of information related to the events of 1869–70 and 1885 is unclear, but she likely drew upon several accounts. While she acknowledges obtaining some of the details from George Ness, Ness was not a supporter of Métis actions. Those who were, such as Joseph and Norbert Delorme, very likely shared some details with Marie Rose or other family members. Marie Rose also would have learned details from her community of both Métis and other pioneers in southern Alberta. Additionally, it is possible that Marie Rose assumed some authorial license to fill in gaps, particularly where she injects dialogue. It is telling that her observation of some of the events refers to the Métis who "ignorantly took up arms against the government," represented by not only Louis Riel, but also by Charlie Nolin. According to Marie Rose, "Nolin had no knowledge of half-breed ways, still he was the chosen speaker."[9] In fact, Charlie Nolin was a Métis man from the Red River area, so might have been chosen for his familiarity not only with Métis history, but with the motivation for the Métis resorting to armed battle with the incoming central Canadian forces. Indeed, as Payment writes, "Nolin was one of the known leaders of the resistance movement. Until May 1885, he had been active within the provisional government." Nolin, much like Louis Riel, had written of the "need to respect and honour their maternal ancestors."[10] Rather than not being aware of Métis ways, Nolin, in "trying to rehabilite [*sic*] himself in the eyes of the authorities" agreed to serve as a witness in the prosecution trial of Louis Riel.[11] Perhaps it was this betrayal that prompted Marie Rose to portray Charles Nolin as an outsider of the Métis community.

For a long time, after the signing of the Treaties, the Red Man[12] could not accustom himself to the White man's civilization. He fretted in the close confines of his house on the Reserve, longing to roam the plains once again and erect his cozy Teepee.

It was not long before, among the young men of the tribes, a restlessness broke out, which later was fanned into open rebellion. In fact there were two rebellions, both of which were headed by a clever half-breed, Louis Riel, and these disturbances are the stories as told to me by my brother-in-law, George Ness, who endeavored, unsuccessfully, to reason with the younger men of the tribe when he saw them headed toward destruction a second time.

It was the first rebellion of 1865 that brought Louis Riel a prominent place in the annals of history. He was a young man of twenty-five years, who had been educated at the College in St. Boniface, thus the Metis had great faith in him, for they felt that he knew White Man's civilization and so could meet them on their own grounds. Their faith proved to be justified for Riel succeeded in securing for every half-breed a scrip of land—240 acres.

But Riel made a very grave mistake, when he permitted the shooting of Tom Scott. Six of Riel's soldiers were chosen for the firing squad; but one of them refused to be a member of such a party, which he declared was really murder and so removed the cap from his rifle before the command to fire was given. Every member of that squad was an expert marksman and at such close range could not have failed in his aim, yet of the five bullets fired, only one struck the victim. He fell to the ground, wounded.

Then one of their number, named Guilmette, stepped forward, drew his pistol and shot Scott in the head where he lay on the ground. The bullet entered the upper part of Scott's cheek and came out through the nose. While still living, he was placed in a rough board coffin. The lid was fastened down and a soldier placed on guard.

From noon until late that night, the wounded man lay in the box moaning and was heard distinctly to say, "For God's sake, either take me out of here, or kill me."

Before mid-night, Lepine, one of Riel's men, removed the lid and with a butcher knife finished him, exclaiming as he returned the lid to its place, "The D--- traitor won't talk again."

For this deed, Scott's friends searched for the leader, Riel, and would have lynched him, but he narrowly escaped and crossed the American border. Here he made himself a home, married and was teaching school, when unrest again seized the Red Men, later fomenting into open rebellion, for the second time.

This second rebellion, is known in History as The North West Rebellion of 1885. My brother-in-law, an Englishman by birth, was at this time a Justice of the Peace and living in Batoche, Saskatchewan.

In the previous year the half-breeds began a series of meetings, discussing their rights and acknowledging their fear of White Man's law. When George heard of these gatherings, he attended them and said, "Brothers, you can't buck the White Man's government, it is of no use to try. They are the Great White

Mother's servants; you are her children. Let us send a message to the Great Teepee."

So they sent their petitions to the government at Ottawa asking for the Indian's right to hunt in the great open plains. But no reply came!

The famous Gabriel Dumont, with a few others said, "We will stir up something; we will make them take notice of us." So they decided to cross into Montana and get Louis Riel, to help them again to secure their independent rights.

At first Riel refused to come back into Canada. He and his family were living comfortably near his little school house, but with the incessant pleadings of his people and his interest in seeing the half-breed retain his rights, he listened to them, and accompanied them back.

At first their only desire was to win through negotiations. Governors Forget and Dewdney were anxious to settle the difficulties before trouble occurred, but now, having gone so far, and not getting any of their terms settled, they were willing to go the whole way, even unto death.

The half-breeds were represented by Charlie Nolin, and several others. Nolin had no knowledge of half-breed ways, [but] still he was chosen speaker with the result that the Metis ignorantly took up arms against the government.

The rest of the story is history. For this and especially the cruel slaying of Tom Scott in the first rebellion, Riel was hung in Regina on November 16, 1885. He walked to his death unafraid, assisted by Rev. Father Andree. O.M.I. Bishop Taché had been very fond of Riel and had known his family well at St. Vital, so in their honor, he gave their rebel son a Christian burial.[13]

In addition to her writing about historical events in her Métis community, Marie Rose was intent on recording the experiences of the pioneers who settled nearby, in southern Alberta. She dedicated an entire chapter to John George "Kootenai" Brown, a character discussed earlier. Indeed, her writing about Brown proved useful to his biographer, William Rodney, who referenced her work. However, while Rodney portrayed Brown as a hero equal to the American Daniel Boone, Marie Rose viewed Brown as more of a rounded character. For example, in Rodney's case, he wrote that "most recollections of Kootenai Brown are highly favourable," while in Marie Rose's case, Rodney determined that she measured him in "feminine terms, painting him in one instant as heartbroken and full of remorse over the death of Olive and in the next breath as a man who neglected Isabella [his Cree wife] and whose eye wandered in the presence of young white girls." Despite relying on Marie Rose's writing, which actually demonstrated that Marie Rose knew Kootenai Brown quite well, Rodney concluded with the question, "Who was present in Kootenai's company to record the significant action or saying or jest, and to preserve it for future use? Obviously, no one."[14]

Marie Rose provided the painful details of Brown's discovery that his first wife, Olive, had passed away during one of his many trips away from home. As Marie Rose wrote, the last wish of Brown's Métis wife was that he would "be kind to the little ones, and put them in some school." Brown honoured that wish, bringing the children to Father Albert Lacombe who was "pleased to grant this last request."[15] According to Marie Rose, after his wife's death, Brown continued with his "wandering disposition." Nonetheless, Marie Rose correctly notes that Brown was the first superintendent of Waterton Lakes National Park, after he "persistently stressed the need for greater conservation measures" of the natural area.[16] Today, visitors to the park can find the site of Brown's grave, where he was buried along the shores of Upper Waterton Lake, between the graves of his first wife, the Métis Olive D'Lonais, and his Cree wife, Cheepaythaquakasoon, who Kootenai and others called Ni-ti-mous, or sometimes also Isabella.[17]

In the following excerpt, Marie Rose provides more details on the circumstances of Olive's death and Kootenai Brown's devastation. According to her, Brown followed through on Olive's wishes by bringing the three children to the Roman Catholic clergy so they would receive care. While some of this excerpt is repeated in other parts of her manuscript, and in this book, it is included here as it expands on Marie Rose's knowledge of Kootenai Brown and tells us more about how Marie Rose arrived at her conclusions about him, such as that he was a somewhat "lazy" man who relied a good deal for his survival on his First Nations wife. It also demonstrates that, despite her knowledge of Brown's failings, she also appreciated his wisdom and his love for the natural areas of southern Alberta.

KOOTENAI

Brown kept a man to do the work around the place while he, each day, rode away on horse back to visit the different detachments, where he just loafed around.

It was while he was on one of these trips that the poor woman died. There was only the hired man to look after her. Poor children; they did not realize their mother was dying, and the farm hand could not keep them away from the cold, breathless body of their mother as they crept round and round her, calling her to awake, crying, "Maman, sleep no more. Wake up!"

The hired man tried to comfort the little ones, but still there was no sign of Brown's return. They looked anxiously for him, day by day, for the woman's corpse could not be kept much longer. While waiting, the man picked up some boards around the place and made a rough coffin. Now to put her in! It was a task. He could never handle her alone, for she was very heavy.

He brought the box into the house, laying it alongside the bed, and tried to roll the body into it, with the blankets wrapped around it. When she finally rolled over, she fell face downwards. Oh, the screaming and the crying of the children as they sobbed, telling the man to leave their maman alone!

Now to take her to the grave already dug! The man tied a rope to the box, and jerked it by the aid of this saddle horse, outside the door, then dragged it to the grave on the brow of the lower lake where she still lies.

Next day Brown came home. As soon as he got off his horse, the three children ran to him, crying, and saying, "My maman is gone," and pointing towards the hill. He didn't understand them, but when he entered the house, the hired man, who was cooking supper said, "Well, Mr. Brown, she is gone! I couldn't keep her any longer, I did all I could. Her last wish was, 'Tell him to be kind to the little ones, and put them in some school.' Then she passed away."

With tears steaming down his face, the hired man burst out, "I never want to see such grief again!"

Brown sat down with his babies around him, sobbing as they sobbed, shaking his head, "Oh, My God, forgive me for what I have done. For being away so long. Forgive me my God. I didn't dream she was so ill. Oh, my God, what will I do. I can never forgive myself. Poor Olive!" So he wailed day by day.

The following day some Stony Indians arrived, expecting to be fed, and what a surprise and disappointment as Brown told them of his wife's death and burial.

There was no rest for Brown after that. Taking his three children he went to Fort Macleod to find the Rev. Father Lacombe to have him place his children in some school. The kind Father knew Olive well and was pleased to grant her last request.

Now Kootenai was a lonely, lonely man. His home was a home no longer and the next few weeks were the most bitter he would ever pass through. Sleepless, he walked the floor, often going to the grave by the lake and talking aloud to his beloved dead.

"Here is where I'll some day lie, beside you, my dear, dear Olive," he would commune. The years have passed, but many old-timers still remember the lovely Indian girl's tragic death.

DEVELOPMENTS

Brown had a wandering disposition. He lived close to nature and loved the natural scenes about him, which were so lavishly presented to him, as he rode his horse

> or fished in the mountain streams. Hunting was his delight, and he enjoyed his trips into Pincher Creek and mingling with the boys. He liked to visit the mill gang, and then he was often heard to prophesy, "Another little drink, boys, won't do us any harm—you know some day, you'll see people flying like birds in the air. These mountains will be a popular summer resort; yes, boys, I see it coming, just the same as I see this liquor in my glass," holding up the tumbler, "and the wild animals will be as tame as you, boys."
>
> Some of the boys would laugh, "Dreams, all dreams, but let us have another little drink and dream again." But his [wife] thought his prophecies pretty smart and called him Man-i-to (spirit).
>
> Brown always dressed in a beaded, buckskin shirt, a stetson hat, and carried a quirt in his hand, which distinguished him from any others.
>
> Since old homestead days, Brown had been game and fish warden, and afterwards was the first superintendent of Waterton Lakes Park.
>
> In 1885, he was a member of the Home Guards, when the rebellion broke out in Saskatchewan. He was a Lieutenant and took his men as far east as Medicine Hat to patrol the country and as he said, to drink Jamaica.[18]

As noted earlier, while Kootenai Brown's biographer William Rodney wrote of Brown as a Prairie hero, Marie Rose saw Brown as a more complex character, who she noted was "rather on the lazy side, yet as long as he had Ni-ti-mous to hustle for him, he was alright." In this longer excerpt below (also referenced earlier), Marie Rose demonstrates her own independence as she encourages Brown's wife to stand up for herself. According to Marie Rose, Kootenai Brown "depended a great deal on his wife"[19] to hunt for him.

In fact, despite that fact that European fur traders did not document the roles of Indigenous women, there is evidence that women have long been hunters. According to evolutionary anthropologists and researchers, in evidence of pre-historic foraging societies across the world, women hunted in seventy-nine percent of those societies. Hunts appeared to be intentional rather than opportunistic, while in "societies where hunting was the most important activity for subsistence, women participated in hunting 100 percent of the time." There is also evidence that women were important in teaching hunting, thus disputing previous claims hunting was determined by gender roles, claims possibly made due to researcher bias.[20] Marie Rose, writing (perhaps facetiously) about Kootenai Brown, noted that he may have starved had he not had Ni-ti-mous to hunt for him.

NI-TI-MOUS

Though Jack Street and Kootenai Brown knew the mountains so well, yet it was on one of these trips, when Street was acting as guide, that he fell over the precipice in a snow slide which I mentioned before in an earlier chapter—and still lies there in his mountain grave.

Street was an ex-policeman, of very quiet disposition. He took part in the rebellion of 1885. He was one of the best hunters I know of, and any time I visited the Browns during Street's life time, there were always quantities of chicken, ducks, geese, deer meat hanging around the walls of the building. Not so after Street's death, for Brown was rather on the lazy side, yet as long as he had Ni-ti-mous to hustle for him, he was alright. Many a sportsman missed Street's guidance on their trips, after his death, and his help with the game they brought down.

Brown depended a great deal on his wife. It was Ni-ti-mous here and Ni-ti-mous there. At any time of day or night, if he wished to start on a trip, he'd waken Ni-ti-mous to go with him. She was a slave for him. He was pretty tricky, as one incident, which I must relate will show.

There were two young girls, who came often to the Brown home and sometimes stayed as long as two weeks for a visit. They used to get Mr. Brown to take them over the mountain routes, sight seeing. Brown had three gentle saddle horses and Ni-ti-mous would put up a lunch for them for the day and away they went. Poor Ni-ti-mous didn't know what was up at first. It kept her busy cleaning and cooking after them. When the three returned from the day's trip, she had everything ready for them to sit down and enjoy.

This went on for several weeks and the girls never offered to help with the work at any time. Mrs. Brown was too simple a creature to consider any ulterior motive and everything was fine for her.

At home again, Brown was the perfect ladies' man and loving husband, as he related incidents of their recent trip.

Then Ni-ti-mous became suspicious, and the girls came once too often to suit her. There was trouble in the camp and she refused to wait upon the girls anymore. Then she put it up to Brown, either the girls left or she did. Brown got into a rage and told her it was alright for her to go, as he thought the girls would stay in her place.

Mrs. Brown told me she prepared to go, though she was broken-hearted. Saddling her horse and taking a few things with her, she left the following morning, coming to our place. Poor woman, a thirty-seven mile trip on horseback in one day, made her very tired by evening.

I was just feed my chickens when I heard hoof-beats upon the ground, and looking up was greatly surprised to see the woman leading her horse. She was too broken up to speak at first, but throwing her arms around me she burst into sobs.

"What's up, Mrs. Brown?" I asked, but she continued her weeping for some time before she could collect herself to tell me her worries.

"Never mind," I answered, "he can't quit you, nor can he marry again. Don't take it so hard. He'll come to his sense some time. That's your home and he can't put you out." But still she sobbed. "You stay with me," I encouraged her, "just as long as you like."

But she really loved this man she was fleeing from. Nor could she eat any of the supper I had prepared for her, but after a hot cup of tea, she unburdened her heart and poured out all her troubles.

After a week's stay, the woman became restless and wanted to move on. Gathering her things together, she set out for Fort Macleod to visit Mrs. Scheers and from there planned to go on to the Hobbema Reserve, if she could find any others going that way.

But her plans didn't materialize. During the week of her departure, things didn't go very well with her husband left behind. The girls' brother, hearing of the flight of Mrs. Brown, went after them, and Mr. Brown lost his girls, his Ni-ti-mous, and all his dreams. Thus he set about to get his Ni-ti-mous back.

Hearing that she was still at Fort Macleod, he went after her. When he entered Mrs. Scheers' house, the first thing to greet his eyes, was his Ni-ti-mous, smoking quite contentedly. Going over to her, he tried to make up for all his mistakes and neglect of her, but she pushed him away and told him to go back to his white girls with their silk and powders. "Ah-wash!" (go away) she said, "I am not good enough for you."

The man tried to reason with her, but Ni-ti-mous was not fooling this time. "Well," he told himself, "the only thing that will bring her back is to present her with a bottle of whiskey, for she is fond of that." But again he was fooled, for she wouldn't drink with him. "No, No, go away," was all she would say.

For three and four days the coaxing went on, but the woman had only one answer, "No, no, go away." But Brown had another plan. "The only way I now have open," he thought to himself, "is to get Mrs. Scheer to help me."

Getting the woman to one side, he made a bargain with her. He promised, "If you persuade my wife to come home with me, I'll give you Ten Dollars." Then he told her of his offer, "Tell my wife, I will give her my bunch of horses and my brand. I will also give her a Bill of Sale in her own name, and a solemn promise never to do again what I have done as long as I live. Tell her I know I have done wrong. I must have my answer by tomorrow. I will call early. Good night!"

> Brown spent the night downtown with the boys having a few drinks, and the following morning, when Mrs. Scheer answered his knock at the door, he exclaimed, "Good morning, sweet lady, what are the results?"
>
> "Everything is alright," she said.
>
> So Mrs. Scheers got her Ten Dollars, Ni-ti-mous got a splendid bunch of horses, a wagon and a load of grub.[21]

While this excerpt demonstrates the independence of Kootenai's partner, it also demonstrates Marie Rose's growing independence and confidence, which emerges in her subsequent writing.

In addition to historical narratives, the archives that hold Marie Rose's personal papers also hold a few short stories that are clearly fictional. One of those, entitled "Does God Know His Business?," focuses on the main character of Georgina, who also demonstrates a growing independence. Georgina does not appear in any of Marie Rose's other writing. More importantly, in this story, Marie Rose relies on these eight main components of a fictional story: character, theme, plot, conflict, setting, climax, exposition, protagonist. Interestingly, there are some similarities between Marie Rose and Georgina: They both suffered loss, and persevered and grew as a result; both of their fathers passed away at a young age, and during the girls' childhoods; both had mothers who re-married; and both were sent away from their families for school. There are, however, key differences: Marie Rose married young; had seventeen children; and was not a world traveler, although she admired those who were. In Georgina's case, she did not marry, enjoyed a career in an office as a bookkeeper and stenographer, and was able to travel, enjoying "many interesting trips."

DOES GOD KNOW HIS BUSINESS?

In June 19—a red-headed eight-pound babe was born to a very devoted young couple who already possessed a little girl three years old. This red-headed babe arrived in one of the worst rain storms of the season, which may or may not account for her being "all wet" ever since.

At three months she was christened Georgina after her father whose name was George. The christening took place at his bedside a few hours before he died from an unattended to acute attack of appendicitis. He did not have strength enough to hold the babe in his arms so he just held her little hand in his while the minister gave the babe her name and sprinkled a few drops of water onto the rusty coloured head.

The death of this young man who was only twenty-nine years of age, left his widow in a very embarrassing situation financially. After settling up the estate she took her babies and returned to her mother's home not many miles away. She remained there until the baby was three years old, when the whole family migrated to the far West, each to take up a homestead. There were the usual hardships of a new country, but the young widow, possessing a happy disposition and a stout heart, managed very well and became dearly beloved by all who came in contact with her. When eventually more settlers arrived in this district, a school was built and little Georgina trotted off to school with her sister.

About the time the school was being built, other buildings were also going up and a general store and post office were erected and an eligible young bachelor was put in charge of them. This young chap became infatuated with the young widow and after a courtship of a few months they were married, much to the disgust of the young widow's parents. They were inclined to think that this girl (for she was still in her twenties) should not crave good times or social life but she should remain at home with her children. However, they soon became reconciled to the marriage. Two years later a young son arrived to add to the happiness of the young couple. The step-father was very proud of his two little step-daughters and was so good to them that they loved him dearly. His happiness seemed complete with the arrival of his son to enlarge his family. The mother, having experienced unhappiness a few years previously, seemed to appreciate this happy life even more than the others and frequently remarked how fortunate they all were.

When the baby boy was fifteen months old, tragedy came into her life again, snatching the young husband away. He had contracted pneumonia while endeavouring to reach home during one of those heavy Western blizzards, rather than remain away from his wife and children any longer than was really necessary for him to complete his business in the surrounding towns. His homecomings were always a great event in the life of little Georgina, who never failed to run to meet him if it were at all possible for her to do so.

It was difficult for her to understand his death and [she] was frightened when her daddy did not answer when she spoke to him as he lay in his little narrow bed, as she referred to the coffin in which he lay. She was a very sensitive child and years later she could recall to memory everything that happened the day of the funeral when they took her daddy away for good.

Again the young matron, widowed the second time, returned to her mother's home, this time with her three children. The baby boy was never a strong child, and little Georgina had sad memories of the nights when she would awaken to find her lovely young mother and Grandmother weeping over her little brother who had taken ill during the night.

It took so much money for medicine, doctors and nurses, that it was necessary for the young matron to move to the city to earn a livelihood for herself and family. She bought a house with her remaining capitol and rented her spare room to High school students who attended the college just across the street. This way she could be at home with her children and at the same time earn money to support them.

Little Georgina from babyhood had a tendency to have bronchial trouble. The first winter in their new home she developed pneumonia and was critically ill for days. During the night she would waken and insist that the nurse call her mother who would come in immediately and sit the remaining long house of the dreary nights, to stroke her brow or hold her hand and hum to her, which seemed to be the only thing that would soothe the child to slumber again.

Georgina was very much interested both in her Sunday School work and day school, and incessantly worried the doctor and her mother to let her get out of bed so she could return to her studies.

When summertime arrived, little Georgina was sent to the country where she would get all the milk, eggs and fresh vegetables she could eat and where she could enjoy God's free sunshine and fresh air. She returned to the city in the Autumn to resume her school work, tanned as brown as a berry, several inches taller and many pounds heavier, much to the satisfaction of all concerned.

Unfortunately however, during that winter an epidemic of Typhoid fever broke out and the three children contracted the disease. When they were well enough to travel it was necessary for the family to move to the country for a time to regain their health. There Georgina was kept out of school for a year. Being a great lover of Nature she spent a great deal of her time looking for bird's nests, watching the mother bird feed her young, and often lending a helping hand so far as the digging of worms was concerned, always hoping that the mother bird really appreciated her efforts. She studied their habits and was so disappointed when the little birds grew big enough to leave their nests. Once a bird leaves his nest he refuses to return and flutters about until his tiny wings develop strength enough to carry his fat little body through the air under his mother's instructions. Georgina's letters to her chums in the city were filled with the wonders of these little birds, the progress of her small vegetable and flower gardens which she tended herself, sometimes pulling the plants out by root instead of the weeds.

Georgina's grandmother gave her a wee puppy one time and they spent many happy hours romping over the meadows together. She had a harness for him and he pulled her all over the farm in a little cart. She called him "Colonel." He developed from a rather awkward lanky looking creature into a very beautiful dog, well deserving the name she had chosen for him. Colonel returned his affection to his little mistress a hundred fold, and guarded her all day long.

Sadness was once more cast over this home when Georgina's sister became ill and after a few months illness, died at the age of fifteen. This was a great shock to the sensitive Georgina. She missed her a great deal as there had always been such a strong bond of love holding this small family together. It hurt her so much to see her mother grieving over the death of her sister. A form of jealousy sprang up and she wondered if it would not have been better if she had been taken instead of her sister. She wondered if her mother would cry as much had she died instead. After a few months however, with the help of her mothers kindness and devotion to her, she overcame this absurd fantasy and grew bright and happy again. If possible, the strong bond of love became stronger than ever between the mother, son and daughter. Possibly small families are inclined to be more devoted to each other than the larger family where the smaller ones are buffeted about by the larger ones and are thus taught to stand up for their own rights or lose out entirely.

Life for a few years was a great struggle financially but each day was filled to the brim with contentment and happiness. At the close of the day there was a never to be forgotten hour when the three would gather around the fireplace and the mother would relate some of the more amusing episodes of her girlhood days and finally end the day with a song in her rich soprano voice. There was a quality in this mother's voice that never failed to comfort Georgina when she was ill or feeling depressed about something.

When Georgina was eighteen her mother managed to send her to a girls' residential college where among her other subjects she studied stenography. She was a bright student and after graduating, soon secured a position as bookkeeper and stenographer. This helped to relieve the financial strain on the mother considerably, whose health was failing her now. She was advised by a doctor that an operation was necessary. This was very depressing news indeed, just when the time had arrived when the mother could relax a little bit and take life easier. Georgina cried herself to sleep many night but always tried to be bright and cheerful in front of her mother. The dreaded day arrived when the mother was to go to the hospital. It was a very sad brother and sister who left their mother in her home at the hospital. There was such a dreadful depressing vacancy around their fireplace that night—the first night that they had ever been separated, and for such a sad cause.

The operation was slated for ten o'clock the next morning. They were waiting in the corridor of the hospital at eight o'clock, unable to be absent longer. When the time arrived they were allowed a hurried good-bye and the mother was rushed upstairs to the operating room. Time dragged very slowly by as they waiting for her return and the minutes seemed hours and the hours seemed weeks. It was such a relief when they eventually saw the nurses and the doctor taking the patient back to her room, where the doctor summoned them and told them that their mother would be all right, the operation had been successful.

Each day they were waiting for the first moment of the visiting period to bgin [*sic*] and by the end of the first week their worries had vanished, mother was improving rapidly so they began to make plans for her return at the end of the next week. It was going to be such fun having mother home again—more pleasant evenings around the fireplace. No more dashing away up to the hospital twice a day, spending money for street car fare that could be ill afforded. They had made so many resolutions that would all add to mother's happiness when they had her at home with them again.

Time dragged on, Mother did not return the second week, nor the third week and finally one day while they were eating their luncheon they received a hurried telephone call to come to the hospital at once. Frightened to death, they climbed into a taxi and dashed madly along, arriving there just in time to meet the doctor on the stairs who informed them that they were too late, "Mother had just died."

It is well said that "Time erases sorrow" because if it were not so we would not be able to bear our grief and heartaches, year after year, if they continued to be as acute as when we first received them.

Without the guiding hand of the mother, these two children felt about as helpless and lost as a ship without a sail. They adored each other and lived for each other, the boy now 15 and the girl 19.

A long lonely year went by, and the world was beginning to look a little brighter. The boy grew to be such a lovely youth over six feet tall now and so manly. He felt it his duty to take the responsibility of the home upon his shoulders. The sister began to depend more and more upon him. She was so proud of him and openly admired him, much to his embarrassment at times. Her happiness now seemed centred around her brother, who sheltered her from all hardships and worry. She continued to work at her stenography but when the day at the office was finished it was such a relief to come home and place the burden of home management etc. on the shoulders of someone else. According to her own analysis she was "mentally lazy" but happy.

However, this happiness was of short duration. One morning, when her brother refused to answer her call, she rose and went into see what was the matter. She discovered that the boy had died during the night in his sleep. The diagnosis after the post mortem was "myocarditis." This great loss was surely unbearable! To have the object of one's happiness, love, very life itself, snatched away so suddenly, seemed to be beyond all endurance.

In utter despair and desperation Georgina turned to her best friend—the minister and his wife, for consolation. This proved to be of little benefit. They were both sympathetic and very kind indeed, but the minister repeatedly implied that it was God's will and must surely be "all for the best," which was certainly not very comforting. He seemed very philosophical over a heartache not his own.

As there must be a motive for every crime, surely God had his motive for taking such a lovely young boy away from one who needed him so much. Perhaps Georgina was just being selfish in wanting him left with her. However, the motive in this case was very difficult to see, but having no alternative, she resignedly agreed that God must know his business.

To readjust herself to a world with the bottom completely gone out of it was a great problem that took a number of years to accomplish. But again Time came to the rescue and healed the wound so that the pain was not so keen but there will always be a sensitive scar.

During the years that followed, Georgina's faith in God wavered occasionally. Sometimes when lonely she would pray to God for help, wisdom and guidance. Sometimes these childlike prayers brought a great sense of comfort to her—other times a feeling of resentment came instead. It is rather a difficult feat to bow to God's will when He alone has taken that which one values most. If it be true that "Whom the Lord loveth he chasteneth," Georgina felt that she preferred less of his love.

The world seemed so vast and unfriendly toward one who was so alone and unimportant. She many times wished that she too could die and join her mother and brother, but realizing that one does not die from grief and also the utter uselessness of such thoughts, she decided to gather the loose ends of her life together and carry on, trying always to remember a saying of her mother's: "We live one day at a time and God never gives us more than we can bear in one day."

She continued her office work for a year and then went in training for a nurse. The life was so different from the life she was accustomed to that once again it was difficult to become adjusted. The work was hard and she was kept so busy during the day that she had no time to think of her own trouble, and at night she was exhausted and would fall asleep as soon as she got into bed, so she had little time left for fretting.

As time wore on, new interests came into her life and her heart ached less for her loved ones. At last her three years of training were completed and she was graduated from her school with reputable standing. A dream that had been nurtured from childhood had at last become a reality.

Having inherited her mother's bright disposition she was well liked by her friends and patients. The hospital itself and nurses' home had seemed like a rest haven for her during her troubled years, but upon graduating she was again faced with the fact that she must meet the world face to face and travel along on her own power.

She took a small apartment near the hospital, applied for private duty at the Nurses' Directory, went home and waited for the telephone to ring to call her on her first case as a graduate[d] nurse, standing on her own feet and earning her own living. As she sat in her own little apartment that first night, eating her first homecoo[k]ed meal in years, a great wave of contentment came over her. She realized that she had been wise in deciding to carry on regardless of the odds, and to try to make something of a life that to her had looked so useless a few years previously.

If we were to view Georgina's life for the following ten years, we would find that they had been very eventful. She was very successful as a "Special nurse," getting all the work she could do. She enjoyed the work and had many interesting cases, both in the home and in the hospital. Home life always appealed to her so much, and many times she would find herself comparing her own happy home life with the lives of the people with whom she came in contact, who seemed to have so much more financially than she had had, but who could not boast about being happier or even as happy as she had been in the all too short years that she had spent with her family and their lack of luxuries.

She had a desire to travel and went on many interesting trips to different parts of Canada and the United States. Her one big trip, and possibly the one from which she derived the greatest amount of pleasure, was her trip across the Atlantic ocean, and the sight-seeing tours she went on while visiting England and Scotland. She kept a diary while on this particular trip and felt that had she any flare at all for writing she could surely write a whole book on the interesting things she saw in the old land.

Georgina is not very young now and although she has never married (which seems to be the one important thing a woman must do to become established), she remains quite happy and is enjoying life to the fullest, in spite of the fact that her chances for ever having grandchildren to whom she could relate her escapades and romances are becoming slimmer every day.

In her more serious moments however, she knows that by being left to her own resources so young, that she has developed more stamina, and self reliance than she ever would have done, had she always had her family to shoulder her responsibilities and shelter her from

> the hard knocks that we are all bound to receive from this old world of ours, and she readily agrees now that "God did know his business."[22]

Marie Rose's intent in writing a short story about Georgina is unclear. Perhaps this story provided an outlet for her own losses and grief. Perhaps it provided an opportunity to reflect on her own resilience as she may have often felt too that she was "left to her own resources so young," when she had objected in vain to her mother's marriage arrangement for her. While we cannot know her motivations with certainty, it is clear that writing meant a great deal to Marie Rose. Her ability to record the experiences of Métis people and the new pioneers that formed her community of connections in southern Alberta were a source of great pride. A letter that no doubt served as reinforcement of her contributions meant enough to Marie Rose that she kept that letter in her papers, which were eventually shared with a public archive. In the letter, a resident of Lewiston, Utah, enquired of Marie Rose about the possibility of an upcoming book.

> Lewiston, Utah
> Nov. 21-1941
>
> Mrs. Charles Smith
> Pincher Creek
>
> Dear Mrs. Smith
> I read your story in the *Lethbridge Weekly Herald*, and would like to buy one of your books, I lived in Alberta 20 years and love to read the story's about the pioneer friends who traveled the prairies in early days.

> I am living in Lewiston, Utah now. Will you please let me know when your book will be published? And the price?
> Yours very truly
> Mrs. Hyrum Ririe
> Lewiston, Utah[23]

Marie Rose was unsuccessful in publishing a book. However, she was successful in having short excerpts published as a series of articles in the Prairie periodical *Canadian Cattlemen*. While those articles were, for a long time, only available as physical copies in the archives, some of them are now available on the online website of that periodical.[24]

In her short story "The Twenty Warnings," it appears that this piece was also intended as fiction. Marie Rose relies on metaphorical writing and positions herself in the third person. For example, in reporting on the news of Louis Riel's return to the North West from his exile in the United States, Marie Rose writes that this "sent a ripple of execration around the land . . . and fell like a cold rain on the ripening harvest of security. Only where the spruce forests of the North Saskatchewan devoured the sunlight was the news devoured like the sunlight was ... in that ill-omened July of 1884."[25]

Marie Rose writes in "The Twenty Warnings" that, despite the petitions on the part of the Archbishop on behalf of "his almost illiterate and nearly destitute charges ... the surveying of lands in question all lands in the North-West Territories will be surveyed according to the system now in force." She then points out the result for the "embittered Métis." While Marie Rose notes the irony of law enforcement at the time, this is where her recounting of events assumes some liberty in that she purportedly quotes from a letter written to Louis Riel by Father Alexis André,[26] asking for his return to the North West. Other references to historical documents confirm the opposite, specifically that Father André had asked that Riel not return. Nonetheless, Marie Rose's political commentary is pointed when she notes the irony of "claim-jumpers" being allowed to deprive the Métis of their lands, but yet if "a half-breed purloined a pair of stockings from the Hudson's Bay store he was punished quick enough, but if somebody trespassed on his land and cut his timber, he was informed that there was no redress."[27]

Marie Rose concludes "The Twenty Warnings" with the events of 1884–85, which resulted in the hanging of Louis Riel, and states that "justice in full, however is still deemed and [*sic*] extravagance." For, as the soldiers for the Canadian government were honoured with medals, "Riel was hanged [and he] died bravely, refusing to resort to the subterfuge of insanity." Marie Rose astutely concludes that the cost of killing "each rebel who had so bravely fought" while those "criminals" who had "brought on the trouble escaped any punishment . . . [was] perhaps the greatest folly of all."[28]

PURLOINED STOCKINGS

This was nothing less than embittering in vain the Metis protested that the system was an inconvenience, an excuse of deprivation of their rights; in vain they protested that the ties of their little farms were dear to them.

Claim-jumpers[29] took advantage of the turmoil. If a half-breed purloined a pair of stockings from the Hudson's Bay store he was punished quickly enough; but if some body trespassed on his land and cut his timber, he was informed that there was no redress, that he had no property rights in the soil or trees. It all seems incomprehensible and unimportant now but to the few half starving Metis then it was a matter of life.

Winters are long on the Saskatchewan, and so were those backwoods men's harangue, it became inevitable that the worried Metis should read their cousin's proclaiment [*sic*] in 1870 should remember Louis Riel a great man, Riel, for had not the government been afraid of him? they would ask his aid again.

And so a deputation was dispatched to Montana to invite him north and if he should hesitate they were armed with a letter from Father André who was later to watch him being hanged saying:

Prince Albert-1884

My dear Mr Riel
The opinion here is so prominent in your favor and longs for you so ardently, that it would be a great disappointment to the people of Prince Albert if you did not come.

So you see you absolutely must come. You are the most popular man in the country, and with the exception of you as five persons, all the world impatiently expects you. I have only this to say. Could come quickly with kind remembrance
I am
A. André

To the school-teacher living in a crowd snakes [*sic*] what could such a letter, such pressing delegation represent but the u [*sic*] the earnest desire of

Providence? So the Spirit of God put him into a conveyance once. It filled him with new hopes, new plans. This time there should be no muddling. This time he would set up a republic. He had always wanted to. And have a proper insurrection and settle all the grievances of the poor Metis, and see to the Indians got back their rights. He will even promise them back their buffalo and then—who knows?—if the government were sufficiently annoyed, they might … [illegible].

The conveyance chosen by the Spirit was exceedingly rickety. And Riel arrives almost too late. The Crees decided upon an insurrection of their own. Left to their simple distractions they … [illegible] groups accustomed to the Police and subsequently to the settlers … [illegible] the feet, but they had heard so much talk about "grievances" that they turned self conscious.[30]

FOLLY

Thirty-five years later this injustice was acknowledged to the survivors and abridged to the extent … [illegible] wilfully, however is still deemed and extravagance.

Riel was hanged after a famous trial at the Police barracks in Regina, and he died bravely, refusing to resort to the subterfuge insolently. Of the [illegible word] some were hanged, some imprisoned or pardoned and all imprisoned—when L. Riel was present, the Canadian people discovered that the … [illegible] of 1884 had cost the lives of thirty three brave men, wounds to one hundred and twenty and a sum total

> thousand dollars a piece to kill each rebel who had so bravely fought.
>
> But the men whose criminal incapacity had brought on the trials escaped any punishment whatsoever—perhaps the great folly of all.[31]

As a chronicler of life stories, Marie Rose was selective in what she chose to record. There may also have been some selectivity in what the family chose to share with the public archive. What was shared with the archives, and reproduced in this collection, supports the designation of Marie Rose as a Métis woman worthy of national recognition, in part due to her role as a chronicler, and in part due to her role as a respected matriarch of her community.

5 — Matriarch

He [Charlie] gave me a wonderful surprise. On one of his semi-annual trips to Fort Macleod for supplies, he returned at the end of two weeks and brought me—yes—a brand new sewing machine. I thought that the world was mine . . . [I] was young, fully of energy and ambitious.[1] *[Working with] two half-breed women . . . with my buckskin work of shirts, gloves and all wearing garments; tents for habitation; cooking in my boarding house; and running a homestead, you will think that I never hesitated to lay my hand to any work that called for my attention.*[2]

WHILE IT IS DIFFICULT TO LOCATE DOCUMENTATION that confirms the critical role that women's work played in the economic survival of early Prairie pioneers, close reading of women's memoirs from the early settlement period, when available, confirms those contributions. While published some time ago in 1984, the stories collected by historian Eliane Leslau Silverman in what is referenced as a "collective autobiography" remain important testimonies of the experiences of pioneer women in the Prairie West.[3]

Compared to the difficulty in locating the written testimonies of pioneer women, it has been difficult to gain a full understanding of Métis women's knowledge. As historian

Nathalie Kermoal writes, "the neglect of Métis women's knowledge is, of course, illustrative of a broader trend. Relatively little research in Canada has been devoted to Indigenous women's knowledge of the environment and of their roles and responsibilities with regard to the harvesting of resources . . . Despite the recognition that both men and women are involved in multiple activities on the land and that these activities are often complementary, most of the work performed by women remains poorly documented and hence poorly understood."[4] This observation speaks to the value of Marie Rose's work in documenting her experiences as a Métis woman who settled on the Prairies and lived over the course of a century, experiencing both the traditional Métis lifestyle and that of a young pioneer wife, mother, homesteader, and rancher.

Here, Marie Rose's writing demonstrates a mature and confident married woman who is proud of the contributions she is making to her family. She is also engaged in the economy of her community, asserting her role as craftsperson for the "check in girl at Waterton Lakes" and doing her "bit for the two great companies." The great companies in this case were the railroad companies for which Marie Rose sewed tents and clothing, as well as the Hudson's Bay Company.

In the excerpt that follows, Marie Rose refers to herself as "Buckskin Mary, the Queen of the Jug Handle Ranch," as she again describes, but in different words, her determination and her independence when she undertakes a journey from southern Alberta to Winnipeg travelling "alone in a democrat with her three boys."[5] In this account of her journey to Winnipeg, Marie Rose writes, at times, in the third person. For example, after writing that "I can remember only one of the many bull teamsters" she writes that "Buckskin Mary Smith, the Queen of the Jughandle Ranch, travelled to Winnipeg alone in a democrat with her three boys."[6] Of course, Marie Rose was not alone with her boys; rather, neighbours joined her. Even so, it was a courageous journey that not many newcomer settler women would have undertaken.

TRAVEL TO WINNIPEG: PINCHER CREEK—JUG HANDLE RANCH

This was the birthplace of fifteen children, two other boys having been born in Manitoba and Montana, which constituted a family of seventeen children, an average family in those days. One night realize what responsibility rested upon the shoulder of these courageous parents when all the requirements and needs in clothing, food, medicine and even doctors were hundreds of miles away. The nearest point for many years was Winnipeg. Then later as Fort Macleod sprung up the toilsome journey was greatly lightened. The town was built on an island, mostly all log shacks, few stores, one general store known as the I. G. Baker and they freighted all their goods in by bull teams from Benton, Montana. I can remember only one of the many bull teamsters and he was George Lavasseur. It was a pretty sight to see these bull teams, long string of them and the teamster popping his long whip. The fear of being robbed of horses by the Indians was cause enough to shudder at the expedition, such realities were in fact too true.

Buckskin Mary Smith, the Queen of Jug Handle Ranch, travelled to Winnipeg alone in a democrat with her three boys, who were hardly out of babyhood in the year 1882, there was a boom in Winnipeg real estate. A man by the name of Jack Bruce, a Scotchman, who was working for Charley Smith had land in Winnipeg and it was his chance to make some money so he hired Charley Smith, my husband, to take him to Winnipeg and offered him one thousand dollars to take him down. This was April 10th, 1882, the snow was very deep but they got ready used a buckboard to carry their bedding, cooking utensils which consisted of a frying pan and a tea kettle and eats. They drove one horse in the buckboard and led two. They were gone all summer and I was left with my three boys and to run the ranch. A hired man by the name of Charlie Barr was left to look after the horses and cattle and he also put in a nice garden. I missed my husband a great deal, in fact I was lost. The hired man beginning to assume too much on account of my youth, I decided, about the end of May, to leave and try to meet my husband between Pincher Creek and Winnipeg. I started to get ready for the trip with my three little boys. I had a democrat, five head of gentle horses, a tent, everything I needed and with a Mrs. McGillis, her son and daughter who were going to Cypress Hills, we left. There was an old man, Joe Brown, who wished to go to Winnipeg so thinking he would be a great help to me I took him along. Joe Brown was a good fiddler and every night we listened to some good old time music. We travelled nicely for about a week and one morning Joe says to us "I believe there is some Indians following us I seen some moccasin tracks when I went after the horses." We were not far from Fort Walsh and we camped early, a nice evening, and we wanted to clean up before we arrived in town.

The next morning Joe went out to look after the horses while Mrs. McGillis was boiling the kettle, and when he returned he brought only the hobbles with him saying that our horses were gone. What a surprise and what luck. The Indians had cut all the hobbles but they left us an old brown mare. Joe took the mare and rode bareback into town to make arrangements to move us on. He was sure downhearted as he only had one saddle horse, a roan, but a peach of a horse. "I'll move you into town then I am going to get my horse no matter what happens. I will go after the thieves in Montana, it's the south Peigan Indians that are doing all the stealing." So he hired a saddle horse, bought a little grub and set out for Montana. So there I stayed waiting for my husband's return, my supplies were very low and I had taken only a few dollars with me thinking I would meet my husband somewhere, turn back and come home but in vain, we could not write to each other, no mail of any kind in those days. I stayed there about a month before Joe Brown turned up with the horses. He got his own, three of mine and four of McGillis', lucky, indeed, to get them back. The next morning Joe asked me how much money I had, I laughed and said only five dollars. "Well, we cannot go very far with that," but Joe had a good gun and was a good shot and we always had lots of wild meat, ducks and prairie chickens. I went to an Indian trader, asked him to let me have $20.00 which he did and I thanked him for his kindness and we continued on our journey. Joe and I and the three little boys went to Batosh [*sic*]. My folks were living there but it took several days to get there. My sister, Mrs. George Ness, had money in Winnipeg so she decided to accompany us bringing her two very small girls with her. She had her own democrat, two horses, but to travel with five small children was no picnic. Of all the trouble we had, no body knows but me. It was the spring of the year and the roads were awful, mud to the hub of the wheel. We travelled until we came to the end of the steel (railroad) on a creek called Flat Creek. Joe then suggested that we take the caboose and go on to Winnipeg and he would take the democrats and horses by land. We had so much trouble, we consented but we did not take any blankets, pillows or clothes only what we had on (young and foolish). The first night in the caboose we did not sleep at all and our little ones cried all night. There were no seats in the caboose. We sat on the floor and spread our skirts (lucky we had oldtime skirts, very wide) and on them our little ones lay all night. There was no rest or comfort for us. Next morning we left for Winnipeg and when we arrived we stayed at the hotel McTavish until Joe Brown arrived with our camping outfit. We then made our camp, rested for a few days before we went to see our grandfather, Urbain Delorme, in the parish of St. Francis Xavier (White Horse Plain). We stayed there two days, returned to Winnipeg, went across the Red River to St. Boniface to see his Lordship Archbishop Tache, who was executor of my father's will. Mrs. Ness drew all her money but I drew fifteen hundred dollars out and bought two fine brown mares, well matched, quiet, gentle to drive. We then started our return journey to the west. After several weeks travelling we arrived at Batoche, Saskatchewan. It was harvest time, my stepfather was cutting his wheat and we stayed there two weeks. My mother hated to see me travel home alone so they decided to come along and I was certainly glad. They also wanted to see the country. When we arrived in Pincher Creek there was a big snow storm but it was just a storm. My husband was sure pleased to see us. I had missed seeing my husband on his return from Winnipeg when I was marooned (you might say) at Fort Walsh. He had been very worried about me and children imagining all kind of things perhaps even murdered by the Indians. He could not sleep, walk the floor all night but we were now home again and happy.

This same year 1882, Remi Beauvais a family from Oregon arrived here with a nice bunch of horses among them being the noted race horse Oceolo, a mare a sure winner and one of the finest horses ever brought into the country. "You bet say" to quote his owner's words. After a few years' racing Oceolo had the misfortune to fall over a dog in one of the races, badly injuring her knees that she never ran again. Mr. Beauvais was a great horse man and took great interest in horse racing.

Also, this same year 1882 Max Brouillet and family came in, settled on Pincher Creek about two miles below Jack Collins and for many years drove the mail between Pincher Creek and Macleod, Macleod and Lethbridge. These two families were very popular as each had nice daughters and good looking ladies were scarce. Many amusing tales are told of the trials and tribulations of these young ladies to keep peace among their many admirers.[7]

At different times, it is evident that Marie Rose was aware that her audience was Prairie newcomers. On these occasions, she refers to some familiar Indigenous customs as "queer." At the time during the fur trade, some Métis women viewed themselves as of a higher class than First Nations women. Their exposure to Euro-Canadian communities, education, and attitudes contributed to this sense of hierarchy.

Yet, Marie Rose's words reflect insights from a chronicler who navigated both worlds—that of the Métis matriarch who traversed the Plains trading with First Nations and the pioneer wife of a non-Indigenous trader and rancher. This dichotomy is evident in her disparaging account of "Indian marriages," as reportedly told to her by the Cree woman who married Kootenai Brown. It is then evident in the words, this time reportedly told to her by Father Albert Lacombe, that Indigenous Peoples were "contented [with] streams [that were] full of different kinds of fish, the country was rich, lots of buffalo until the white people came and started the treaty. It was the worst thing."[8]

ADVENTURES OF THE WILD WEST

> The laws of the Indian. For instance, if any of the women would fall in love with another Indian, another wife's man, if caught, they would cut off that nose which would disfigure her for life. The buck (male) they would tie up to a tree and lash him for three days until almost dead. The moral law was very strict. Thou shalt not covet thy neighbor's wife. The chief's word was law and for which, the tribe has the greatest respect. They loved one another but had an abhorrence of death. If one of the relatives died, the [women] would cut off one of their braids of hair and scrape her leg with a

knife until it would bleed. If a chief would die, they would put up the best teepee, arrange all his belongings in side as if he were alive, even prepare a fire but not light it in the centre of the teepee, place the pots and pans around the fireplace, make up his bed with the very best blankets, then they would sit him up in life position at the door of the teepee. They would shoot his favorite horse so he could ride him to the Sandhills. That was one tribe's belief. Another tribe believed that if they would put a body high on a rack, it would come to life again. They were a queer people,[9] but they were happy wandering over the Prairies. Some Indians worshipped the sun; that is the reason they had Sundances.[10] The Sundance was a supplication to the sun to grant special favours such as prosperity or to cure sickness, &c. To conduct this dance, the tribe would choose a woman and a man with a good, moral reputation; -- There was very little friction between the Indians and the authorities but it was found necessary to put a stop to certain dances held among them, particularly the Ghost Dance and the Sundance. (The Sundance as it held today is greatly modified.) ...

... The government stopped all those cruel ceremonies. The Sundance is still held but much modified. The time of year this dance is held is when the saskatoon berries are ripe & so as to make their berry soup. For months ahead whoever is to conduct this dance must gather tongues (buffalo), it is a special dish and each attendant gets a small piece. A date is set for this dance and there are Indians from all over attending. They gather in a place where they can get trees to mount their tents and where there is good water. The tents are placed in a circle with a big medicine tree all decorated with different gifts they give to the sun, in the centre. Inside they have a little apartment for the medicine man with a whistle. He is almost naked, a skin around his shoulder, his body and legs are painted. He comes out to look at the sun whistling and dancing. In one corner are the drummers beating the tom-toms and singing. The one who conducts this ceremony does not eat or drink for three days and they keep the celebrations up for a week. They all dance in a circle, the women in one and the men in another. They are dressed in their best beaded dresses and suits and headdress. These dresses and suits are made of the best and finest buckskin (not smoked) and also white elk skin, beaded most elaborately in designs in the most beautiful colors and fringed. The headdress is made of eagle feathers and falls below the knees. They, during these dances, gave gifts to each other. The gifts consisted of horses, nice blankets, bead work on purses and bags, anything they thought that was worth giving. Indian life is free and easy and they are very seldom sick. The [women] would have their babies without any doctor and would never remain in bed and some would give birth to a child while travelling. If you would observe two [women] stopping behind the others, when travelling, you could imagine what happened for when they arrived in camp there was a new baby. The Manito, the Great Spirit, looked after them. Their medicine were roots that they dug. There were some great medicine men and women among them. They built a round sweat house, making a hole in the middle. The frame was made of willow sticks and covered with buffalo hides so no steam could escape. It was large enough for two to crawl in. They heated big rocks in the fire until red then rolled them into the house in this hole. They then poured cold water over these red hot rocks, you can imagine the steam that rose from those rocks. They crawled in and you could hear them making all kind of noise, groaning and singing. After they came out they would go to the lake or steam and jump in. It did not seem to hurt them, in fact it was healthy. They claimed they had a sure cure for rheumatism and bone diseases. In a buffalo herd, there are always some old animals, too old to keep up with the rest, generally old bulls, so they killed the animal, opened him up quickly taking the insides out and stick the sick man or woman in. They said it cured but it would be an awful hard thing to stand. They have cured their cripples that was and good many imaginable ways.

Years ago most of the Indians had nothing but a travois with dogs. They would load these travois with their belongings and a dog would pull them. They would walk. These were the very poorest. If one should have a horse or two, he was a big man, a very rich man. This was the real Indian life of the Plains. There were better times for them when the I. G. Baker Co. and the Hudson's Bay Co. came into the country as these companies did a lot of trading with them. The men from these different companies took [Indigenous women] for wives and that's where the half breeds originated from.

The [women] would have to do all the work while the bucks did the hunting and smoked their pipe. The [women] with a papoose on their back would have to put up the lodges, get the wood and water, cook the meals and make the dry meat. After the buck killed his game, he would lie down and take his comfort. The [woman], the poor slave, did the work but never grumbled. They respected their men and called them "Nina," Big Man. There was never any love making, no courting among them. If any young couple was fit to marry, the parents would choose the mate, no marriage ceremony. They would tell them to go together, whether they loved one another or not, it made no difference. They had to obey their parents. The Indians count the winters for one year, also the moons they count for a year. So many moons make a year.

Mrs. Kootenai Brown often told about the Indian marriages. She would say, "No good, no good." She was married to a buck and had eight children by him. He was a lazy no good husband & used to beat her up and she carried a mark on her head from a blow from him. She could relate many thrilling tales of Indian life. She liked the white people the best; white man is good, Indian life, dog life.

Father Lacombe claimed the white people spoiled the Indians. Civilization did not agree with them. They were happy roaming the Plains, hunting for wild game. They were contented and happy living mostly on wild meats and fish. Streams were full of different kinds of fish, the country was rich, lots of buffalo, until the white people came and started the Treaty.[11]

Marie Rose wrote from the perspective of a Métis matriarch who engaged in buffalo hunting and trading and had knowledge about First Nations culture, but also as a settled pioneer. As a mother, she felt it important to write about how they (and she) cared for the children and, it is here, that she highlights the importance of Indigenous knowledge: "Indians are not fools. They are nature's best scholars."[12]

From discussing moss as a method to keep a baby dry and comfortable, to hammocks made of ropes, Marie Rose shares with pride the extensive knowledge that allowed her to establish herself as both a mother and matriarch. At the time, European beliefs and practices around gender were emerging, and "patriarchy as a pattern of gender and family relations" was in full swing.[13] According to Diane Payment, Métis women were often called "Une femme en vaut deux (strong like two people)." As she notes, "work, work, and more work" was "their motto. In addition to changing moss bags (baby carriers in which moss acts like a diaper) and feeding and clothing large families, they had the skills to live independently or survive on the land because men were often absent—'visiting,' hunting, trading . . . They were the traditional healers, midwives, and counselors, skills that they passed on to newcomers."[14]

Beyond the memories of her time as a young girl, and of her skills as a matriarch, Marie Rose moves into a discussion of the roundup of cattle that no doubt reminded her of the buffalo hunts, noting that "it's a beautiful sight to see several thousand head of cattle bunched together."[15] This was no doubt reminiscent, for Marie Rose, of the thousands of buffalo that lived on the Plains before the transitional period when the fur trade gave way to a more sedentary and agricultural lifestyle.

Then he goes among the animals and rides around them, when one buffalo folows [*sic*], the coaxer bellows like a buffalo, the rest then follows and he rides to the entry of the corral and gets the buffalo to go in. There are riders behind making all kinds of noise to keep the herd going in the same direction. When all the buffaloes are in the corral, they drop a gate made of heavy poles. The Indians then get on the top of the corral and start their killing, mostly with bow and arrow as there are very few guns and very little ammunition among them. What guns they have are flint lock guns. That was the main reason they built buffalo ponds [*sic*; pounds], the animals fell in, one piled on top of the other and they would all be killed. Brown was well posted on Indian life.

The Indians made their bows and arrows out of chock-cherry wood and twisted sinew, making them very strong with a flint rock end. They trim the flint rock to a sharp point so it can pierce anything that is shot. Indians are not fools. They are nature's best scholars.

I must mention how the [women] took care of their infants; they would make a bag with buckskin strings to lace it, and they would gather moss in swamps in sacks full, which they dried and put next to the baby. The baby is quite comfortable in this moss as it is nice and soft. Preparing the moss for use—they put it in pans and heat it, if there are any insects in the moss, the heat drives them away. They had no washing to do as they used moss. For baby's powder, they used rotten wood pulverized very fine. As the baby grew older, they made a wooden frame with a bag attached laced with strings. They would put the baby in this bag and they could stand the frame up anywhere or the [woman] would strap it on her back and keep on working. If anyone would study early Indian life, they would wonder how they stood the hardships. They were always in the sun, bare headed, no wonder they are called the red race.

How we raised our babies in early days—we very seldom took our babies up and held them, no rocking nor fussing with them. I always had a hammock made of two ropes, stretched by a piece of rawhide then we would put a blanket between the two ropes and a pillow. We never took the baby out of the hammock to feed it, we would stand near the hammock. When through feeding, I would give the hammock a push and go back to my work. The baby would go right to sleep again for many hours. We also used what we called a baby bag, laced with strings, into which we put the baby. When we untied him, about three times a day, the little fellow would stretch for all he was worth, and kick his little legs generally about a half an hour, then he wanted to be tied up again. In the morning after his bath, he wanted his bag and hammock. The reason we used these bags, we had no safety pins in those days.

Roundups in this country in early days were looked upon as the big events of the season. The spring roundup began some time in May. Stock men, cowboys and rider from different parts of the range joined together. They chose a captain, then loading up the mess wagon with grub, cooking utensils and bedding &c., they started to the south end of the ranges across the Kootenay River which was usually high at this time of year. There

> were sometimes five or six outfits together, each with a camp cook and tents to accommodate all hands, making a village of tents. They made a horse corral of their ropes and set the wagons in a circle. When the herders brought in the horses in the morning, each wrangler caught the horses he needed for the day. Round-ups are hard on men and horses. It is a great time for breaking broncs. Great fun for the lookers-on, no doubt each man had his turn. In the morning the riders would strike off in every direction, as the cattle were gathered in from every part of the country. It's a beautiful sight to see several thousand head of cattle bunched together and the riders riding around until they get to one of the corrals. The stock association had built several corrals in different parts of the range.[16]

In her description of the practices of settler pioneers, and considering her own knowledge of traditional medicine, First Nations people have similar practices. For example, McClintock observed, among the Blackfoot women, expertise around medicinal uses of roots and herbs.[17]

Indeed, it was not only working with traditional material, such as buckskin, that Marie Rose relied on as she established herself as an important community member, medicine woman and midwife. As Kristin Burnett wrote, "Aboriginal women performed important health care functions in their communities—well into the 1930s." Even the adoption of Western medicine by Indigenous women "did not signify cultural disintegration; rather, it was a pragmatic response to changing social, economic, and political conditions." It also "served as a means of cultural exchange between Aboriginal people and Euro-Canadians, especially the women of both groups."[18] In the interviews conducted by historian Nathalie Kermoal, many Indigenous women noted, "Although our nokoms did most of the doctoring, every mother had her own stash of medicines used for croups, coughs, fevers and any number of childhood illnesses." As Kermoal also notes, "For more serious illnesses, however, a woman who had earned a reputation as a healer [such as Marie Rose] would be consulted" with "Métis healers" sometimes travelling many miles to gather the plants needed for their healing practice.[19] According to her granddaughter Jock Carpenter, Marie Rose always traveled with a buckskin medicine bag filled with "pouches of herbs, tea drinks, and poultices."[20]

Recognized as a healer and as a matriarch, Marie Rose also enjoyed recording the "sociable times" she shared with her community. She wrote that she played the violin to accompany her neighbour and Prairie character Kootenai Brown. When he sang the traditional song "The Red River Valley," she sometimes called him a "very interesting raconteur."[21] This was a song familiar to the Red River Métis, including Marie Rose and Kootenai Brown's first wife.

It is significant that Marie Rose wanted to record all the verses of this traditional song. It is also interesting that this song was the very one that Marie Rose broke into at the end of her interview with H. G. Baalim, in 1956, at the age of ninety-six years. While Nathalie Kermoal is discussing the need for Métis women to be active participants in the process of securing their rights to the land,[22] it is also true that Métis women as active participants were, and continue to be, affirming their collective identity. It is striking that Marie Rose was, as early as the 1940s, an active participant in this transmission of identity, well before the affirmation of Métis as Indigenous Peoples in Canada, when she determined to chronicle her life as a Métis woman on the Prairies.

RED RIVER VALLEY

We often went to visit Mr. and Mrs. Brown. Charley would bring a jug and a few bottles to treat them. Many times in their conversation, Brown would say to us, "I see the future coming. In these mountains and sceneries, some day you will see a town in here, a resort, we may not see it, we are getting old. You will see steamboats running on these lakes. I have had my day. I feel satisfied to die and be buried along side of my first wife. She was a good woman. Ni-ti-mous is good too." We spent many good times with them, Brown was a comic. While we were having a sociable time, he would suggest songs and his favorite song was the "The Red River Valley," thinking of his first wife. He was a pretty good singer and I would play the violin.[23]

The Red River Valley.

It's a long time, you know, I've been waiting
For those word you never would say
But, alas, all my fond hopes have vanished
For they tell me you are going away.

CHORUS.

Then consider awhile ere you leave me
Do not hasten to bid me adieu
But remember the Red River Valley
And the half breed that loved you true.

II.

They say from this valley you are going
We will miss your bright eyes and sweet smiles
For, alas, you take with you the sunshine
That brightens my pathway awhile.

CHORUS.

III.

Will you think of the valley you are leaving
How lonely and dreary 'twill be
Will you think of the heart you are breaking
And be true to your promise to me.

CHORUS.

IV.

When you go to your home cross the ocean
Will you think of those bright sunny hours
That we spent in the Red River Valley
And the soft shade of its bowers.

CHORUS.

After singing awhile, he would turn to his wife, Ni-ti-mous, what about making a cup of tea. In no time tea would be ready and he would say come good people come and eat. He would then suggest to go and set the nets. This was in the winter and the next morning we would have all kinds of fish. In the summertime, he would take us in boats fishing. He was a live wire, always on the go. He would say "Come, Charley, another little drink won't do us any harm. I have kept my boots undone so as to be ready to kick them off with my last dying kick. I have had good times and bad times in this world but I am quite satisfied. I know my days are numbered."

On his second homestead, across the river he raised all kinds of tame rabbits. Mrs. Brown made several

> rabbit robes and received good money for them. Brown was a very interesting raconteur, one was how the Indians would slaughter the buffalo.—Out of big logs, they would build a round corral, very high, and at the entry, they built wings on each side the same height as the corral the buffalo generally run in single file, one after the other so the coaxer dresses himself with a buffalo robe made for the purpose, the head with horns.[24]

As Marie Rose explains in this excerpt, "no trip was too hard for us pioneer women." While clearly enjoying the socializing with neighbours, Marie Rose felt pride in doing her "bit for the two great companies." It is significant that she wrote about this in several instances in her documents that have been preserved by a public archive. In this case, she was referring to the Hudson's Bay Company (HBC) and the Canadian Pacific Railway (CPR). "Hiring two half-breed women," Marie Rose set up her small cottage industry, sewing tents not only for the company but for new farmers. As she notes, the buckskin work involved in making "all wearing garments" in addition to "running a homestead, you will think that I never hesitated to lay my hand to any work that called for my attention."[25]

Marie Rose hired the two Métis women to fulfill contracts for companies such as the CPR and HBC, as well as for settlers and the tourism sector, and demonstrated her ability to establish a cottage industry that was critical to not only her own household economy, but to the growing settler Prairie economy. The fact that Marie Rose was able to establish herself as a businessperson and property owner in the southern Alberta area at that time was a rarity, not only because she was female, but also because she was Indigenous. In her manuscripts, Marie Rose writes briefly about a neighbour in Pincher Creek who many referred to as "Old Auntie," another example of the rarity of female businesspersons at the time. This woman was Annie Saunders, who worked briefly as a nanny for Colonel James MacLeod. Not unlike Marie Rose, Annie's accomplishments as a businessperson were also remarkable. As Cheryl Foggo writes, Annie Saunders was a "Black woman—who had almost certainly spent the first 30 years of her life enslaved." Foggo managed to find "dozens of references to Annie scattered in old letters, old news-papers, memoirs of Pincher Creek visitors and residents" to determine that Annie Saunders eventually operated three businesses, including a laundry, a boarding house, and a restaurant.[26] While she does not refer to "Old Auntie" in the following excerpt, Marie Rose shares with obvious pride memories of her own work that contributed to her family's survival.

MAKING TENTS

When the Canadian Pacific Railway was in the course of construction near the foothills, the company wished to buy tents from the Hudson's Bay Company, but there were not enough on hand to supply them, so I was able to do my bit for the two great companies.

Tents were needed right away, and of different sizes, and when the boss of the outfit came and asked me to make the tents, I felt it a big responsibility but I decided to do the best I could.

The Companies were to provide me with all raw materials, ropes, thread and the necessary canvas. It was lucky for me that I had my sewing machine, as I entered this new venture for I had never made such a thing and was not sure if my work would be satisfactory.

To begin with I had an order for two dozen tents, and as agreed, the necessary canvas was brought to me; or perhaps it should be called heavy duck of eight to twelve ounce size. Hiring two half-breed women, who laid out the duck, cut it into shape and did the hand sewing, I worked at the sewing machine, stitching long seams all day; from early morning until we couldn't see on account of the dark. Besides this, cooking had to be done for my family and my help, but in time it was finished to the satisfaction of the Company, who brought me more canvas and ordered another dozen tents.

After completing that three dozen tents, I vowed I would never again make any more, for the heavy material, the heavy lifting and the heavy sewing were very tiring; but later I made tents for farmers to use in their hay fields.

So with my buckskin work of shirts, gloves and all wearing garments; tents for habitation; cooking in my boarding house; and running a homestead, you will think that I never hesitated to lay my hand to any work that called for my attention.

It was while on the homestead that I had my first run away. I had gone into town to get a supply of groceries. By this time, there were many settlers in the west and fences formed a boundary line around each ranch, which necessitated the opening of gates—a terrible drag to all oldtimers, who had been accustomed to go for miles upon miles without the barrier of barbed wire.

My ride to town was uneventful and as I had a quiet team I could leave them as I opened and shut the gates

> that barred my way. But on the return journey, the horses must have been too anxious to reach home, for as I closed the gate, that shut the main trail from the town road, they forgot to wait for me.[27]

Although Marie Rose noted that "Charlie was boss," she was independent and added to the context of the growing rights of women. As she related on several occasions, Kootenai Brown was fortunate to have his Cree wife to hunt for him. The longer excerpt below, that was discussed earlier, is also included here because it demonstrates that Marie Rose herself perceived it as important. She encouraged Brown's Cree wife to stand up for herself. It suggests that, despite acknowledging that Charlie was "boss," Marie Rose did not fully ascribe to a patriarchal worldview that was imposed by the Roman Catholic Church, which was involved, to some extent, in her identity formation. As more European settlers arrived on the Prairies, too, colonial and imperial ideologies influenced the expectations of male and female roles. While she is focusing primarily on non-Indigenous English-speaking women in this particular study, Sarah Carter's *Imperial Plots: Women, Land, and the Spadework of British Colonialism on the Canadian Prairies* provides a detailed examination of the restrictions placed on women's independence.[28]

Marie Rose was confident in the rights of Indigenous women, despite the imposition of patriarchal views by incoming Euro-Canadian settlers and the federal government's oppressive legislation, the Indian Act of 1876, that limited the rights of women. The patriarchal views of the Roman Catholic clergy, given their relationships with the Métis people, were important as well. As Jacinthe Duval notes, the Roman Catholic church "saw the Métis as the raw material for a new Francophone prairie culture." Duval adds that "the dynamics of Métis identity construction were shaped by men conflicted by their ambiguous views of this mixed-blood culture."[29] Marie Rose revered the Roman Catholic clergy. Yet, she appreciated her role as the matriarch of her family and her independence that she proudly wrote about her ability to provide for her family, both while Charlie was alive and during her time as a widow.

NI-TI-MOUS

> She was a slave for him. He was pretty tricky one incident. I must restate, I won't mention the name of two young ladies, I got this from Mrs. Brown she says those two young girls would come up to have good time with from Brown some time two weeks at the time to go & see mountain scenery. Brown would get three gentle saddle horses. Ni-ti-mous would put up the lunch for them for the day, away they'd go. Poor Ni-ti-mous did know what was up at first. She would do all the cooking and cleaning after them. She'd have everything ready, when they'd get back. This went on for few weeks. She never mistakes anything, when they'd get back, everything was O.K. The girls never offer to help at all, always with Brown letting, laughing, telling each other what they'd seen and what they haven't seen, what lovers do. Ni-ti-mous commence little suspicion, they come up once too often for to suit her, give her lots of extra work waiting on them. Pretty soon war in the camp, she wasn't going to wait on them no more, she was

> leaving if they . . . wouldn't go home. Brown in rage told her, all right, she could go, thinking that the girls would stay and have his good time all right. Ni-ti-mous, I'll get ready & go broken hearted She saddle her horse, took few things with her, she left the next morning, head for Charly Smith Ranch; poor woman rode all day, thirty seven miles, to get there in the evening. As I was feeding my chickens, who should I see [but] Mrs. Brown leading her horse, she came to me and kissed me started to cry. I was surprised, what's up Mrs. Brown. She kept sobbing; when she got through crying, she up & told me what had happened. Well, Mrs. Brown, never mind, he can't quit you, he can't get married again; don't take it so hard, he'll come to his senses some time, that's your home he can't put you of. You stay & visit with me stay as long as you like with me. So we went in and made her a good supper. She was so broken-hearted she couldn't eat anything, only drink a cup of tea. That night she told me all her troubles. After a week stay she got lonesome.[30]

Clearly Marie Rose grew to be a confident and capable matriarch of her own Métis family and community. Indeed, with Charlie's death in 1914, Marie Rose carried on as a widow for forty-six years—a lifetime really.

6 — Widowed Homesteader

[After Charlie died] I was left with very little, a few cows and horses after the mortgage companies got theirs. I thought I would take a homestead in the south country, thinking I would make a living for the rest of my children. I had three girls and one was not very healthy. I left my girls in town to run the house, I had two boarders, and that brought me a little money. I would go to the homestead a week at a time, I put in a small garden and I would come back and forth.[1]

MARIE ROSE STAKED A SECOND HOMESTEAD in 1915 after Charlie had passed away, and she was only able to do so because she was a widow, serving as the head of her household, and because her contemporaries considered her to be non-Indigenous. As Sarah Carter explains, the reserve system and the Indian Act that governed the lives of "Indians," meant that they could not obtain land off a reserve. On the reserves themselves, there was no ownership of land, "although 'location tickets' to small plots were issued to males who could pass these down to heirs . . . Women came into possession of location tickets generally only as widow."[2] Indigenous women, such as Marie Rose, had to grapple with non-Indigenous widows when they sought to stake a homestead of their own. Yet, as Carter notes, there were many hurdles for all widows who sought to purchase land. Widows had to have minor children dependent on them, and they had to reside on the homestead for six months of each year for three years.[3] Marie Rose was able to earn her patent on this homestead in 1923 as she continued to operate the boarding house in Pincher Creek. However, it is not clear how much income she ever garnered from that homestead.

When Marie Rose took the second homestead, her three boys had just enrolled to serve in the war in Europe. Unfortunately, two of those sons were killed in action. As she wrote,

> *How can a mother stand all these misfortune[s], lost two sons at the first war, had to send a nice girl to school in east, she died in Valleyfield convent. Out of seventeen children, I [have] only five left. 1952 Lost another son killed in a tractor horrible death.*[4]

This sentiment is shared by Marie Rose in an undated page of notes that immediately follows a longer excerpt which appears to be re-copied by Marie Rose from a newspaper report. This report detailed the tragic accident that took the life of her son Michael, who had been "riding the rails" from Pincher Creek to find work. Like many young men of the time, Michael had hopped onto a freight train, hoping to jump off at another location where he might find seasonal employment. This was a risky undertaking and many young men were injured or lost their lives before reaching the promises of a better life and finding a way to support their families. While it appears that Michael had obtained a ticket for this part of the journey, the practice of illegally "riding the rails" was a North American custom for many young men and women, particularly during the Depression era. Some estimates claim that two million men and "perhaps 8,000 women" became a class of citizen often referred to as "hoboes."[5] By late 1932, when one in four Canadians was out of a job, an estimated "more than 400,000 people," Canadian officials determined to enforce the Railway Act to prevent the dangerous practice as "hundreds of transients, or hoboes, could be seen riding on top, underneath or hanging on to the sides of boxcars . . . many lost life or limb when they fell off or under moving trains."[6]

It was before this particular loss, though, that Marie Rose wrote of the "first great sadness to enter our home" in 1897. This is when she lost nine-year-old Mary Anne, who Father Albert Lacombe had encouraged Marie Rose to send to a convent school in Quebec. In the same excerpt, Marie Rose spoke of the year 1914, which "brought many sorrows." It was the year that she lost Charlie, her "comrade of thirty-seven years." It was also the year that she lost her eldest boy to illness, and the year that she describes her "greatest sorrow," when her three youngest boys "proudly entered the house wearing red ribbons on the lapels of their coats." They informed their mother that "their country has called them to war." Though only two of the boys went overseas, neither returned, as both died on the same day. Marie Rose concludes this excerpt with the sad sentiment that "seventeen children [were] now reduced to six!"[7]

WIDOW BOYS

The first great sadness to enter our home came in 1897. Up to that time, there were no schools in Pincher, so

Rev. Father Lacombe was instrumental in entering our nine-year-old Mary Ann at the Convent of the Holy Names in Valleyfield, Quebec. All went well with her until the last week in November, we received this kind but heart-breaking letter:

"It is my painful duty to give you the details of poor Mary Ann's sickness and death. It was all so sudden that we could not warn you of the danger that threatened her life. She was taken sick with croup on November 18th and breathed her last the following morning. She did not seem to suffer, and said she was glad she was going to see the Infant Jesus.

"Last Sunday, she brought a new white dress the Sisters had given her. 'Do you want to wear that dress in winter, Mary Ann?' the Nun asked. She smiled saying, 'yes, yes.' Poor child she did not imagine then, it would be put on as a shroud. Enclosed is a letter begun just a few days before her death.

"This morning, when the pupils were told of her death, many of them burst into tears."

So we lost our first little girl, many miles from home.

1914 brought me many sorrows. In the spring, my husband, my comrade of thirty-seven years, died; but there was one consolation for me. He died in the Faith. It had been my constant prayer through all those years, so surely I dared not grieve too much.

In June of the same year, my eldest boy came from Montana for a visit; while here he became very ill and died, leaving behind him a wife and three children.

But my greatest sorrow came when my three youngest boys, proudly entered the house wearing red ribbons on the lapels of their coats. When I looked up and saw that I cried, “No, no, boys, you can't”! It was the cry of mothers heard over the world when their men folk come home to break the news that their country has called them to war.

“Now, mother,” soothed Jonas, standing so straight in the hour he had heard his country's call, “Canada needs us”! I shall not weary you with the details of the arguments that followed, suffice it to say that day by day, from the window of my town house, I watched those boys march by; laden down with their heavy knapsacks, but strong, virile, the pride of many a mothers' heart, and when they returned, foot-sore and weary, while their officers rode along, still fresh on their fine horses, I grieved, “We have not learned democracy yet.”

I don't care to dwell upon the day we were summoned to meet in front of the King Edward Hotel to say good-bye to our boys. You went through the same thing in your town. As Pincher Creek is two-and-a-half miles from the station, the boys had to march that distance to entrain for training at Calgary. We mothers, too, went to the station and the last I saw of two of my boys was a waving handkerchief from each of their hands.

Though three of my boys enlisted, yet but two went away overseas, for I had written to headquarters asking for the release of one of my boys, as I needed him to help me work my homestead, which I had taken after the death of my husband. So they sent back my youngest.

I divided my time between the farm and the boarding house in town. My three girls assisted me in town and when the last letter came from the boys that they

> were proceeding overseas, I wrote to army headquarters with the result I just mentioned.
>
> How can I write of that awful day, August 15, 1917, when one exploding bomb claimed the lives of my two heroes. There were no more cheerful letters to receive, only the memory of those waving handkerchiefs as the train pulled out of Pincher Station; and how can I tell of the awful, tearing loneliness, when later the Armistice was signed and my boys could never return with those whose homes were blessed by their re-union.
>
> Seventeen children now reduced to six![8]

When Marie Rose lost her husband, she noted that she was "left with very little, a few cows and horses after the mortgage companies got theirs." It was at this time that she decided to take a second homestead. As noted, while unmarried or Indigenous women could not take homesteads, as a widow, the Homestead Act permitted Marie Rose to do so. No doubt the fact that she was "left with very little" prompted Marie Rose to seek that second homestead.

However, this second homestead for Marie Rose clearly did not yield the living that she hoped. It also, unfortunately, served as the location where she learned that she had lost two of her boys who died fighting in Europe in the First World War. In the excerpt that follows, Marie Rose agonizes that she had "never dreamed that [she] had raised boys to go to so cruel a war." It was in 1917, while at the homestead, alone, that Marie Rose learned of the loss of her sons. She concludes this section of her manuscript with the words "I am alone in this world." She was not physically alone, of course, as she continued to live with family members until her death in 1959. However, the grief that she re-lived as she wrote about her losses no doubt led her to believe that she was truly alone.

ALONE

In February 1914, my husband, Charley Smith, died and a little later my oldest boy was also laid to rest. I was left with very little, a few cows and horses after the mortgage companies got theirs. I thought I would take a homestead in the south country, thinking I would make a living for the rest of my children. I had three girls and one was not very healthy. I left my girls in town to run the house, I had two boarders, and that brought me in a little money. I would go to the homestead a week at a time, I put in a small garden and I would come back and forth.

When the war broke out in 1914, I never thought for a moment that any of my boys would answer the call to arms perhaps because I had not yet realized they were men, always thinking and calling them boys. One afternoon the three boys came home wearing a red ribbon on their coats, I was a broken hearted mother. I never dreamed that I had raised boys to go to so cruel a war. They tried to explain, to make me understand that they had to fight for our country and if they came back they would have seen a part of the world. Just what so many of our Canadian boys thought, an adventure. They were not the only ones. Many, many mothers sacrificed their husbands and sons as well.

This was in August, a military unit was formed here and training began. I will never forget those days as long as I live, my feelings were so hurt. They used to march past the house driven like a bunch of sheep, loaded down with their knapsacks, marching for miles, and the officers riding fine horses. The poor soldiers with sore feet having to march just the same.

The time came for the boys to leave and go to Calgary, to continue training. Oh, how I felt when they all marched in front of the King Edward Hotel. Parents flocked together to try and see their loved ones and from there they marched to Pincher Station. The boys were allowed to have a few minutes with their parents and when they bid us good-bye, tears were streaming down our cheeks and we were choked with sorrow. Watching that special train pull out, we stood there dumbfounded and blind with tears, watching white handkerchiefs waving in every window as far as we could see the train going, it was hard after nursing those boys from babies, raising them and to see them go, never to return, a cruel world. While they were training in Calgary, the three boys wrote me regularly. When they wrote and told me they were leaving for across the sea, the old country, I could not bear to see the three go. I wrote to the head officers and explained that I needed the youngest boy, to discharge him and send him home, two were enough to sacrifice. I needed one boy to help me to improve my homestead so they sent home the youngest of the three.

On August 15th, 1917, while we were at the homestead, came the sad news that my two boys were killed. It gave me such a shock I took sick with grief. Oh my God, what affliction for a mother to stand. When my boys wrote home, they never mentioned the hardships they were enduring in the trenches and at the firing line, they were men.

When the armistice came and the war was over, again a fresh wound in my heart, when some of their companions returned, oh dreadful feelings, when I learned from those men how hard it was to struggle against hardships and death in the trenches and along the fighting line. I will never forget that awful wicked war. Surely some day God will bless us for those afflictions. I still carry a sore spot in my heart, will carry it to my grave. I am seventy-six years old and it does not seem very long since I raised those seventeen children and held them to my bosom. My happiest days were when they were all small, contented to see them around me, working for them and laboring for them. A day will come when we will meet again.

Today I have six children alive, three girls and three boys, all married.

I am alone in this world but it won't be for long then my adventures will end.

God bless us all.

[Written in handwriting: *"Mary Rose Smith passed away April 4th, 1960 in St. Michael's Hospital Lethbridge. Buried in Pincher Creek April 7th at the age of 98 yrs."*][9]

While not physically alone, the deaths of her sons in the war, and that of her son Michael while he was "riding the rails" clearly remained with her. In an age when there was no modern technology to store documents, Marie Rose chose to memorialize the loss of Michael by re-copying what was most likely a newspaper article shared with her. It is perhaps a fitting tribute to this widow's memories to share that re-written article in its entirety.

—INSTANT DEATH—

Instant death in a most horrible manner. Michael Smith from Pincher Creek falls from train. Mangled remains picked up near city, inquest opens today.

A fatality of an unusually gruesome nature took place, Friday morning on the CPR tracks between Hosmer and Fernie, As No. 213 pulled into the depot shortly afternoon it was noticed that some of the wheel and journals of several coaches bore blood marks, and other indicative of an accident of serious nature. The matter was reported to the authorities and in a short time Coroner Wilkies, and several C.P.R. men were on the way to Hosmer in a special consisting of a caboose and engine.

Remain Found

The train proceeded slowly and at several places along the track could be seen traces of the fatality. After going about three miles the searching party came upon the remains of a full grown man torn out and mangled almost beyond recognition. Almost opposite from the Wood McNabb mill was the location. The remains were carefully gathered together and brought back to this this [*sic*] city where they were sent to Scott undertaking establishment to await the action of the coroner's jury and to be prepared for interment as soon as his relatives can be located.

Identification Made Easy

The clothing of this unfortunate man were searched in hopes that some thing might be found that would furnish a clue to his identity. A memorandum book was found in his pocket giving the name of deceased as Michael A. Smith and his post office address as Pincher Creek, Alta. It also added that his occupation was a rancher, near the aforesaid post office. Further search of the book contained the desired information, that in case of accident, Mrs. C. Smith of Pincher Creek should be notified. The name of Smith was also scratched on the metal clasp of a belt which deceased wore around his waist.

Conductor's story

Conductor Cavin of the train when asked about the accident, he stated the man had boarded on Monday morning and that he had noticed nothing peculiar about him; he tendered a ticket for Fernie to which place he was presumably going.

The last conductor Cavan [*sic*] saw of deceased he was standing on the platform between two of the front coaches, the conductor remarked that the deceased had better go inside as standing on the platform was prohibited but evidently the warning was not heeded. No motive can be advanced for Smith trying to leave the trains at the point where his body was found and it is probable that the actual circumstances surrounding his untimely death will remain a mystery. Smith was a well built man apparently about 25 or 36 years of age.

Coroner Wilkies has sworn in a jury who viewed the remains and adjourned until next week when the regular inquest will be held. (had evidently been here before.)

Another leaf of the book contained the names of the following places. Fernie, Reford, Columbia Falls, Kalispel [*sic*], and Polson which would seem to indicate that his business called for a visit to these places or that it was a memorandum of places visited in the past. Mrs. C. Smith of Pincher Creek has been notified of the mishap as requested in the memorandum book.

How can a mother stand all these misfortune, lost two sons at the first war, had to send a nice girl to school in east, she died in Valleyfield convent.

Out of seventeen children, I only five left.

1952. Lost another son, killed in a track, horrible death.[10]

7 — Pioneer of the Plains

MARY HELENE PARFITT WROTE OF HER MOTHER Marie Rose and about the skills she learned "at her Mother's knee . . . beading, cooking with native roots and herbs, tanning skins, making soap, drying meat."[1]

Jock Carpenter wrote of her grandmother Marie Rose that she

> *let it be known that she would take in boarders and ladies-in waiting. Women, feeling that their time to deliver was near, moved into the house . . . Marie Rose's midwifery, carried on while she was at the ranch, increased now that she was in town. The Indians too, came to town as they had done on the ranch, seeking treatment for eye infections. Boiling a herb the way Mother Gervais taught her, Marie Rose bathed the infected eye with the cooled liquid and soon the redness and draining disappeared . . . Marie Rose had put in many years of midwifery and the doctors were disgruntled at not being called to deliver the babies. Soon Marie Rose had a letter from officials in Edmonton telling her that she must desist from the practice.*[2]

The pioneer practice of relying on First Nation and Métis midwives has been discussed earlier. According to Marie

Rose's daughter, her mother eventually received a letter from officials advising her against carrying on with her midwifery. However, pioneers to the Prairies had long availed themselves of Indigenous midwives. According to Burnett, "some doctors appreciated the expertise of Aboriginal midwives." Burnett refers to the oral testimony of Harriet Sayese, "a midwife who lived near Frog Lake" and who related that "when people were sick, mother was called on to help, often being midwife. She even helped Dr. Miller at times, as midwife, in the old hospital he had set up in his home at Elk Point in the early 1920s."[3] Burnett's research demonstrated that "as late as the 1930s, many settler women in the West preferred Aboriginal healers and midwives to hospital care."[4] Burnett, when writing of Marie Rose and with reference to her manuscripts, confirms her familiarity with Indigenous medical treatments. Burnett also found examples of Euro-Canadian settlers referring to these treatments, but often not acknowledging who they acquired this knowledge from, suggesting that the anonymity of their sources served claims by early settlers of being "real pioneers."[5]

For Marie Rose, the pioneers of the Plains, the "oldtimers," were the fur traders and buffalo hunters. As a chronicler of the transitional times for the Métis, Marie Rose was recognized by the local newspaper upon her passing with the headline, "South Alberta Pioneer passes in Lethbridge." That a newspaper would recognize the passing of an Indigenous woman in 1960 is not only unusual, but it is telling. It speaks to the impact that Marie Rose had on her community—an impact that has only recently been recognized by historians and others. Her family, though, recognized her significant contributions. They determined to preserve Marie Rose's documents in a public archive.

Indeed, Marie Rose Delorme Smith has now been recognized as a person of national historic significance by Parks Canada, with the details of her historical contributions listed as "Métis rancher/homesteader, medicine woman, author." As the designation reads, Marie Rose

> *exemplified the leadership of a Métis woman. During her long life, she saw the fur trade economy and culture of the prairies shift to the more sedentary and increasingly agricultural economy . . . she successfully ran her family's ranch and established a small cottage industry in a pioneer town, while still continuing her Métis culture and skills by serving as a medicine woman and midwife. She also owned her own property at a time when few Euro-Canadian women, and even fewer Indigenous women, were able to do so. As an author, she is a rare example of a Métis chronicler of the roles of Métis women during the fur trade, buffalo hunting, and homesteading periods, and of the cultural change on the Prairies.*[6]

Marie Rose was recognized as a pioneer, and that article is worthy of sharing in its entirety. At various times, newspapers featured stories of Marie Rose, again speaking to her stature as both a pioneer and a Métis matriarch.[7]

Another local newspaper recognized Marie Rose's contributions, not only as the creator of traditional documents, but as a chronicler, noting that she "has a fund of stories of the early days":

> *Their first home was a long one-room log cabin. Open house was kept at the Smith home with never a hungry white man or Indian begin turned away. Here also on the*

homestead were born 15 children (17 in all) . . . Mrs. Smith is expert in beadwork, working on buckskin, and has made countless beautiful beaded gloves, jackets, moccasins, etc. She has a fund of stories of the early days.[8]

In a longer article written by Marie Rose's neighbour Emma Lynch-Staunton, she recounted the story of Marie Rose's life from the "Romantic Meeting" to the time she "Settled at Pincher" and concluding with the story of her "Large Family."

EIGHTY YEARS ON THE PLAINS: THE STORY OF MRS. CHARLES SMITH, PINCHER CREEK[9]

By E. Lynch-Staunton

A pioneer of eight years standing. Mary Smith (Mrs. Charlie Smith), as she is known to her hundreds of pioneer friends, is writing the memoirs of her life on the western plains and her book may shortly be given to the public. Interesting reading it should be of the adventures, romance and hazards of the life she lived, and of tales of her pioneer friends who have been a part of that great opening up of the prairies stretching from the Great Lakes to the Rocky Mountains.

Just eighty years ago on October 8, 1861, Mrs. Smith was born at White Horse Plains in Manitoba. She was baptised Mary Rose Delorme at the little church of St. Francois Xavier near the present site of the city of Winnipeg. Her grandfather was an early French voyageur and fur-trader. Her father was born in Winnipeg, her mother being Marie Des Marias of the

Cree Indians, whose father was Scotch, an employee of the Hudson's Bay Company.

Her grandfather attained great wealth as a trader. He had wide lands, hundreds of head of horses, and Red River carts and wagons for freighting. He built himself a fine house, "Just like millionaire," says Mrs. Smith. Her father followed in the same business of trading and hunting buffalo across the plains but he died young. Mary was sent to the convent at St. Boniface to be educated. Her mother and the family rejoined the Cree traders and were constantly travelling across the prairies hunting and trading. She married the second time, Gervais, who freighted goods from the Hudson's Bay Company headquarters to Edmonton, Ft. Pitt, Ft. Carleton, Duck Lake and Rocky Mountain House, and returned with furs for the company.

A Romantic Meeting

They were camped on the prairies when she met her husband. He had come from Winnipeg with a big outfit of horses and wagons loaded with trade goods, who while camping overnight had lost their horses. They assisted them in finding the animals, and as they had recently killed a bear and so had plenty of meat, and the newcomer had a "permit" and the wherewithal for celebrating, the whole camp went on a tremendous jamboree.

Charlie Smith was of Norwegian nationality but he was born on a ship in the Mediterranean Sea. At the age of twelve he was a sailor. How he became a western trader is not told. He was the typical adventurer and daredevil, tall in stature, fair of skin, with blue eyes and light-colored hair that he wore long. It is said he was scarred from head to foot from brawls and encounters with Indians and traders all across the prairies. When he set eyes on his future wife, who was only sixteen at the time, he declared, "That's the girl I'm going to have!" and forthwith gave over a hundred dollar bill to her mother for the daughter. He produced a fine cariole piled with fur robes and ringing with bells, and they proceeded to Edmonton and were married by Father Lacombe at St. Albert.

Settled at Pincher

For as long as the buffalo lasted they travelled the prairies freighting furs and goods back and forth to Winnipeg camping in sheltered winter quarters or dawdling across the wide prairies during the summer months. They followed the last of the buffalo to Montana and there her husband bought 250 head of cattle and brought them to Alberta to where they took up their ranch on Pincher Creek. Their brand was the jug-handle (a loop in the brisket), and the ranch was known as the "Yughandle ranch."

They also had from two to three hundred head of horses. Her husband was tremendously big-hearted, open-house was absolutely the order of the house. He could drink with the best of them and was a wild rollicker.

On his death in 1914 of pneumonia, Mrs. Smith proved herself an astute business woman in building a comfortable home in Pincher Creek where she retired, and which has since been a home for many old friends. Father Lacombe was a friend and adviser all through her life.

Among their neighbors were many notable pioneers, among them Judge Ives L. Brooks, J. C. Routhler, L. Gareau, Lewis Hamond, A. B. Wilmot, A. E. McCulloch, the Nicols, R. Duthie, L. Hirondelle, H. Riviere, Kootenay Brown, Wm. Gladstone, McGillis the fiddler; Sam Sharpe, and many others, about all of whom Mrs. Smith had something to tell in her book.

A Large Family

Her family consisted of seventeen children but only six are now living. Two sons, Jonas and Theodore, gave their lives at Vimy Ridge. Dick [?] also joined up for the Great War but was too young at the time to go overseas.

There are three daughters Ellen, Mrs. Parfitt, Lethbridge; Jose, Mrs. Burke, Moose Jaw; Eva, Mrs. Forsland, Edmonton. Her sons are, George, at Seattle; Robert, in Montana; and Dick and his family at Pincher Creek.

Mrs. Smith learned the art of Indian beadwork when she was a girl and makes beautiful articles of buckskin beaded and embroidered in most artistic designs, such as buckskin shirts and coats, belts, moccasins, and gauntlets. These she is glad to sell.

The amount of sorrow that Marie Rose endured was also documented in the local newspaper, which recounted the loss of both of her sons in the war in Europe.

PINCHER CREEK HARD HIT BY THE WAR THIS WEEK[10]

Four of Our Gallant Sons Make Supreme Sacrifice
Two Well-Known Families Bereaved
Tom and Bob Sharp and Jonas and Theodore Smith Give Up Lives in Our Behalf

Pincher Creek has indeed been hard hit by the war this last week. The news was received last Thursday that Tom and Bob Sharp had been killed in action, on Friday Mrs. C. Smith received word that her son Theodore had made the supreme sacrifice and as we go to press we learn that she has received another telegram announcing that her other son Jonas had also been killed.

It is with heavy hearts that we record the death of these gallant lads. Tom and Bob Sharp were the sons of Mr. and Mrs. R. Sharp, formerly confectioners here. Tom was on the Echo staff about three years ago and was a very bright boy. The father is a sergeant in France and Mrs. Sharpe is at present in Vancouver. Our sympathy goes out to her in this hour of trial.

Jonas Smith enlisted with the 192nd battalion and was well-known in the district. It is hard to think that the grim reaper should visit these families so soon again.

The sad news was received by Mrs. Smith, on Friday last, that her son Theodore had been killed in action.

A gloom was cast over the whole community when the news of the young heroe's [*sic*] death was noised around. He was a fine strapping young lad and it is hard indeed to feel he will not come back.

He joined the 13th M. R. and left for overseas with that unit.

The sympathy of the entire community goes out to the bereaved family in their hour of sorrow.

Conclusion

Métis girl, young bride, chronicler, matriarch, widow, homesteader, pioneer, medicine woman, and now a national historic figure. She referred to herself as "Buckskin Mary" and "Queen of the Jughandle"—all-encompassing terms that demonstrate that Marie Rose Delorme Smith understood her history, owned her identity, and forged her own path that expanded well beyond pre-determined boundaries and expectations imposed by a changing society.

It is only fitting and appropriate that, as we have been privileged to engage with her voice in this study, we read from Marie Rose's great-grandson Donald McCargar, on the opening pages of this book, his words of how Marie Rose's life story impacted his own. As Donald writes, the journey to embracing a Métis identity has not always been straightforward and taken for granted. Indeed, the story of the Métis in Canada is complex while inspiring. Donald writes about sharing his pride in his Métis identity with his own mother, who remained hesitant throughout her life to embrace that identity herself.

Although Marie Rose did not reference "Otipemisiwak," the people who own themselves, by reading her words one gets the distinct sense that chronicling her life story and those of her community was very much about "owning herself." Emerging as a strong, independent, and resilient matriarch and pioneer was not a foregone conclusion when Marie Rose ran "like a wild antelope" to escape Charlie Smith's proposal. Pleading with her mother to understand that she had not accepted Charlie's proposal, only to have her mother confirm the marriage arrangement, would not have precluded for Marie Rose, the young girl, that she would grow to own her life and her destiny. That young girl would not likely have envisioned a day when she would have her words published, a day when she would set out on a nine-hundred-kilometre journey across the Prairies, a day when she would set up a cottage industry to ensure she always had "pocket money" for her children, a day when she would set out on her own to work her homestead for weeks at a time, leaving her girls to operate her boarding house.

Identities for most people are complex, none more so than for a Métis woman "coming into her own" on the Prairies in the early 1900s. As a Métis girl, Marie Rose understood her father to be a man of some material wealth. She understood her grandfather to be a man of some importance in the Métis homeland in the Red River, a man referred to as "le Chef des Prairies." As a young girl, Marie Rose also understood that her world was changing. The buffalo were dwindling, and the roles of the Métis as Wardens of the Plains were transitioning. When her father died and she was sent to a convent to be educated by Roman Catholic nuns, Marie Rose recognized that the education she received would serve to prepare her for this changing world.

Although she protested her mother's marriage arrangement, Marie Rose would also have soon recognized that forging a connection with a non-Indigenous robe and whiskey trader who appeared to be of some wealth was an important connection, particularly in a changing world. It was a connection that would afford her a position as an important community member in the new settlement of Pincher Creek in the southern Prairies. While clearly a racialized woman who necessarily continued to rely on her Métis community, culture and identity to survive and to thrive, marriage to a non-Indigenous man enabled Marie Rose to assume a position of some status. The somewhat fluid boundaries on the Prairies when she was first establishing herself as the matriarch of her own family ensured success, so that as boundaries became more rigid, she could continue to enjoy that success and status. However, ensuring that success required that she be astute and flexible in the presentation of her own identity.

For Marie Rose, at times, she clearly perceived that maintaining that status required that she assume some racist ideologies, if not privately, then certainly publicly. Marie Rose would have been acutely aware that her world in the early 1900s would not be seeking out the written words of a Métis woman on a regular basis. Her writing was a novelty in her Métis world, and it certainly was in the emerging world in which she navigated her identity and status. Marie Rose's positionality as the wife of a non-Indigenous fur-trader–turned–rancher afforded her the opportunity to chronicle the stories of her new community. Her positionality as a racialized woman informed her presentation as one who appeared, at least in her written words, to hold some Indigenous Peoples in disregard. Yet, that presentation of

Indigenous Peoples as "other" and "lesser than" could not sustain itself in the bulk of her manuscripts. For the most part, Marie Rose demonstrated an admiration for and, in fact, an important and beloved kinship with Indigenous Peoples. Even more importantly, for the most part, Marie Rose demonstrated a pride of identity as a Métis woman who had extensive familial, trading and community relationships with both Indigenous and non-Indigenous people. Her desire to chronicle her life story and the stories of those in her extensive network can only demonstrate a pride in self, a pride in culture, and a pride in identity. It can only demonstrate a confidence in the roles that she created for herself and that she owned—homesteader, wife, mother, businessperson, author, pioneer. It can only demonstrate a confidence and pride in the all-encompassing role of Métis matriarch that she embodied and embraced.

Acknowledgements

As I reflect on this book, I am incredibly grateful for the opportunity I had all those years ago when I first encountered Marie Rose's story in the archives held by the Glenbow Institute Archives (now the Glenbow Western Research Centre). I can recall spending hours and hours engrossed in her words, being drawn into her story. The more I engaged in those words, the more I came to view Marie Rose as a kind, intelligent, empathetic, capable, and strong woman. I grew to admire her for all of her abilities, but even more so for her passion to engage and to make a difference in her world. Like so many women born in 1860, Marie Rose did not enjoy all of the options that she would have if she were born in a different era. Yet, in many ways Marie Rose forged her own path. She chose to establish a small cottage industry, she chose to open her home to new pioneers, she chose to serve as a medicine woman and a midwife, she chose to operate a boarding house, she chose to work on a second homestead as a widow, and she chose to record her memories in writing. Many years later, her family chose to share those written stories with a public archive. They also chose to share their own memories of Marie Rose and, in doing so, enriched our knowledge of this important Métis woman.

Donald McCargar is the keeper of many of the family photos and stories shared with him by his mother, Shirley-Mae McCargar, Marie Rose's granddaughter. Donald has been as kind and generous as his mother was upon our first meeting. He remains a steadfast friend and supporter of my desire to always learn more about Marie Rose. His stories, and those of his mother, contributed to the recognition of Marie Rose as a person of national historic significance by the Historic Sites and Monuments Board of Canada, Parks Canada. The fact that Donald has shared his thoughts in the foreword to this book have not only blessed me and my work, but it is my belief that this act of generosity would make his mother and great-grandmother very proud.

Thank you, maarsi, Donald, Shirley-Mae, and most importantly, thank you Marie Rose, for your dedication to recording your memories so that many would learn about the important contributions that you, and so many like you, have made as a way to ensure that your Métis culture and identity would survive.

Notes

FOREWORD

1 Donald McCargar was likely referring to family oral histories, specifically that the Jughandle Ranch had earned a reputation as a spot for days-long drinking events.

2 As the newly-formed dominion of Canada attempted to secure its borders from coast to coast against the expansionist vision of the United States, the North-Western Territories and the Hudson's Bay Company–controlled Rupert's Land were amalgamated to form the North West Territories and transferred from the United Kingdom to Canada in 1870. This vast new territory spanned, at its largest, much of the land between northwestern Quebec and Ontario (around the Hudson Bay) to British Columbia and Alaska. The territory would eventually and progressively be re-divided to form the present-day borders of the provinces and territories of Manitoba, Saskatchewan, Alberta, Yukon, Nunavut, and the Northwest Territories.

INTRODUCTION

1 Parks Canada, "Marie Rose (Delorme) Smith National Historic Person (1861–1960)," accessed October 15, 2023,

https://parks.canada.ca/culture/designation/personnage-person/marie-rose-delorme.

2 Heather Conn, "Cuthbert Grant," *The Canadian Encyclopedia*. Historica Canada. Article published January 30, 2028. Last edited January 25, 2023.

3 Jock Carpenter, *Fifty Dollar Bride: Marie Rose Smith, A Chronicle of Métis Life in the 19th Century* (Gray's Pub., 1977).

4 Doris Jeanne MacKinnon, *Metis Pioneers: Marie Rose Delorme Smith and Isabella Clark Hardisty Lougheed* (University of Alberta Press, 2018).

5 Marie Rose Delorme Smith, "The Adventures of the Wild West of 1870," Glenbow-Alberta Institute Archives (hereafter, GAIA), Box 1, File 3, 48.

6 Sarah Carter and Patricia A. McCormack, eds., "Lifelines: Searching for Aboriginal Women of the Northwest and Borderlands," in *Recollecting: Lives of Aboriginal Women of the Canadian Northwest and Borderlands* (AU Press, 2011), 5.

7 Carter and McCormack, "Lifelines," 9.

8 Doris Jeanne MacKinnon, *The Identities of Marie Rose Delorme Smith: Portrait of a Métis Woman, 1861–1960*, (University of Regina Press, Canadian Plains Research Centre, 2012). See also: MacKinnon, *Metis Pioneers*.

9 Carter and McCormack, "Lifelines," 8.

10 Sarah Carter, "The Montana Memories of Emma Minesinger: Windows on the Family Work, and Boundary Culture of a Borderlands Woman," in *Recollecting: Lives of Aboriginal Women of the Canadian Northwest and Borderlands*, ed. Sarah Carter and Patricia A. McCormack (AU Press, 2011), 212–14.

1 Marie Rose Smith, *Eighty Years on the Plains*, GAIA Box 1, File 4, 1.

2 Doris Jeanne MacKinnon, *The Identities of Marie Rose Delorme Smith*, 134.

3 Smith, "The Adventures of the Wild West of 1870," 1.

4 At various times, Marie Rose refers to Indigenous Peoples as "Indian." Historically, this term was used to describe Indigenous Peoples in Canada, mostly First Nations. Today, it is derogatory. When Marie Rose was writing, its use was common.

5 The "White Horse Plain," located in Manitoba, was incorporated as St. François Xavier in 1880. Still known locally as White Horse Plain, the name was derived from a First Nations story of a white horse that roamed the area after the deaths of a young Cree warrior and his would-be bride. Rich in buffalo and other animals, the area was a source of food and fur for First Nations and Métis. It was also previously known as Grantown, after Métis leader Cuthbert Grant. This area is where Marie Rose's family had lived for generations. Rural Municipality of St. François Xavier, "A Brief History of the RM of St. François Xavier," accessed April 11, 2025, https://www.rm-stfrancois.mb.ca/p/history.

6 The Greater Prairie Chicken is now extinct in the southern Prairies but at the time that Marie Rose settled in southern Alberta, they were plentiful. The prairie chicken is "culturally significant to the Siksika (Blackfoot) and the Plains Cree First Nations in Canada, and lives on in their prairie chicken powwow dance." Erin Jamas-Abra, "Greater Prairie Chicken," *The*

Canadian Encyclopedia. Historica Canada. Article published January 25, 2023.

7 Pemmican was a staple for many Indigenous Peoples. Métis produced pemmican for their own survival on the trail, but also for sale at fur trading posts. Pemmican was important enough to the Métis economy that a short-lived Pemmican Proclamation, forbidding the export of food supplies, almost led to a war between the government troops and the Métis. John E. Foster, "Pemmican Proclamation," *The Canadian Encyclopedia*. Article published February 7, 2006, last edited July 23, 2015. Accessed July 2, 2025, https://www.thecanadianencyclopedia.ca/en/article/pemmican-proclamation.

8 There were different names for this product that became a staple of the Métis economy. Often, the names depended on the ingredients. For example, "taureaux" might refer to sacks that were treated with fat and others might be treated with berries or other fruit. The word "pimikan" was a Cree word meaning "manufactured grease." Manitoba Métis Federation, "Pemmican," accessed May 1, 2023, https://www.mmf.mb.ca/Métis-minute/pemmican. "The Manna of the Plains," was Marie Rose's reference to her Roman Catholic faith and the manna bread believed to have been sent from Heaven for the Israelites.

9 Smith, "The Adventures of the Wild West of 1870," 1–5.

10 Ibid.

11 Diane Payment, *The Free People—Li Gens Libres: A History of the Métis Community of Batoche, Saskatchewan* (University of Calgary Press, 2009), 206.

12 Marie Rose was likely referring to her great-grandfather Francois Delorme, who travelled west from Quebec. Her grandfather, Urbain Delorme, was born in the North West and was Métis as Francois Delorme had married an Indigenous woman.

13 "Makoons" is an Ojibwe term meaning "bear cubs." Nora Livesay and John D. Nichols, eds., The Ojibwe People's Dictionary, accessed April 11, 2025, https://ojibwe.lib.umn.edu/main-entry/makoons-na.

14 The Dakota (Sioux) have lived on their territories since before 1200 AD in what is now western Ontario and eastern Manitoba. After the War of 1812, although they moved closer to what is now the United States, they never abandoned their northern territory and today some remain in Manitoba and in Alberta as part of Treaty 6 territory. Peter Douglas Elias, "Dakota," *The Canadian Encyclopedia*. Historica Canada. Article published December 12, 2010. Last Edited March 02, 2017, accessed June 2, 2025, https://www.thecanadianencyclopedia.ca/en/article/dakota.

15 Marie Rose refers to this game as "Change Hands" but correctly notes that many Indigenous Peoples engaged in "Hand Games." These remain a vibrant part of Indigenous cultures. Michelle Filice, "Dene Games," *The Canadian Encyclopedia*. Historica Canada. Article published December 5, 2016. Last edited November 10, 2023.

16 Smith, *Eighty Years on the Plains*, 2–6.

17 Smith, "The Adventures of the Wild West of 1870," 7.

18 Parks Canada, "Fort Garry—Fort Edmonton trail National Historic Event," Directory of Federal

Heritage Designations, 1989, accessed September 29 2023, https://www.pc.gc.ca/apps/dfhd/page_nhs_eng.aspx?id=1588.

19 Marie Rose's reference to the "Blackfeet" could be the Confederacy which includes Siksika (Blackfoot), Kainai (Blood), Piikani (Peigan), Stoney Nakoda, and Tsuut'ina (Sarcee). See Alex Tesar, "Treaty 7," *The Canadian Encyclopedia*. Historica Canada. Article published August 19, 2016. Last Edited November 10, 2023, accessed June 2, 2025, https://www.thecanadianencyclopedia.ca/en/article/treaty-7.

20 Marie Rose may have been referring to the Battle of the Belly River in 1870. While most of the existing publications of this battle are written from a colonial perspective, and the site of the battle was recognized as a national historic site (with the wording of the commemoration currently under review) a recent virtual reality project brought together the voices of Indigenous Elders to share their stories. See: Kris Hodgson-Bright, "Battle of the Belly River," YouTube, 2024, https://www.youtube.com/watch?v=3auWH4uxjGA.

21 Marie Rose spelled her husband's name two ways: "Charley Smith" and, later, "Charlie." "Charlie" is used on documents found at the Kootenai Brown Pioneer Historical Village and in Land Title Registries.

22 Tail Creek was a vibrant community when Marie Rose wintered there. Also called Boss Hill, in the central part of what became Alberta, was used as a winter settlement by Métis families including that of Francois Gabriel Dumont. The community existed

between 1870 and 1879 with an estimated population of between 1,500 and 2,000. It served as a staging area for the Métis from as far north as Lac La Biche, Lac Ste. Anne, St. Albert, Edmonton, and east to Batoche, as well as a major distribution point for free traders. When the North-West Mounted Police travelled from Fort Edmonton in 1875 to visit the Tail Creek Settlement, they reported four hundred cabins, a community hall, and timber works there. All that remains now is a cemetery preserved as a historical site. In 2013, the area known to Marie Rose as Hobbema, and home to four First Nations, officially adopted its Indigenous name of Maskwacis.

23 MacKinnon, *The Identities of Marie Rose Delorme Smith*, 129.

24 Smith, *Eighty Years on the Plains*, 7–10.

CHAPTER 2: ENCOUNTERING CHARLIE

1 Smith, *Eighty Years on the Plains*, 69–71.

2 Susan Sleeper-Smith, *Indian Women and French Men: Rethinking Cultural Encounter in the Western Great Lakes*, (University of Massachusetts Press, 2001).

3 Smith, *Eighty Years on the Plains*, 65.

4 Payment, *The Free People—Li Gens Libres*, 95.

5 Rupertsland Institute, *Métis in Alberta: Métis Foundational Knowledge Theme* (Rupertsland Institute, 2022), 54–56.

6 William C. Wonders, "Far Corner of the Strange Empire: Central Alberta on the Eve of Homestead Settlement," *Great Plains Quarterly* 3, no. 2 (Spring 1983), 93.

7 Smith, *Eighty Years on the Plains*, 67.

8 Along with repetitions in Marie Rose's writing, there are small errors too. Marie Rose was at the convent two years, not four.

9 Smith, *Eighty Years on the Plains*, 64–67.

10 Brenda Macdougall, Carolyn Podruchny, and Nicole St-Onge. "Introduction: Cultural Mobility and the Contours of Difference," *Contours of a People: Métis Family, Mobility, and History*, ed. Nicole St-Onge et. al. (University of Oklahoma Press, 2012), 13–14.

11 Smith, "The Adventures of the Wild West of 1870," 11.

12 This is a reference to Pincher Creek, along which Marie Rose and Charlie settled on the Jughandle Ranch.

13 Marie Rose was not an orphan. Although her father had died and she had attended a convent school, she lived with her mother, step-father, and all of her siblings. Her use of "orphan" may have been a way to indicate her feeling of abandonment because of her arranged marriage.

14 This paragraph demonstrates Marie Rose's stream of consciousness when writing. While reminiscing about her early married life, Marie Rose explained the presence of her brother, also named Charlie. Smith, "The Adventures of the Wild West of 1870," 9–11.

15 Smith, *Eighty Years on the Plains*, 171.

16 Smith, *Eighty Years on the Plains*, 65.

17 Smith, *Eighty Years on the Plains*, 162.

18 Marie Rose calls Annie Saunders "Old Auntie," who was a Black woman. Saunders—an important pioneer—originally came to southern Alberta as housemaid to Colonel James MacLeod of the North-West Mounted

Police. She eventually established herself as a proprietor of several businesses, including a laundry, restaurant, and boarding house. See: Cheryl Foggo, "Assembling Auntie: Illuminating a long-forgotten pioneer," *Alberta Views: The Magazine for Engaged Citizens* (January 1, 2009).

19 In referring to "fry cakes" Marie Rose may have meant a fried bread, which is similar to bannock, typically baked over an open fire.

20 Smith, *Eighty Years on the Plains*, page number.

21 MacKinnon, *Metis Pioneers*, 455.

22 Smith, "The Adventures of the Wild West of 1870," 74–75.

23 Smith, "The Adventures of the Wild West of 1870," 67.

24 MacKinnon, *Metis Pioneers*, 455.

25 Marie Rose openly discussed that Charlie engaged in drinking and silly, racist antics, and is likely an indication of the struggles that she faced, and what she wanted readers to understand. These examples support her many sentiments expressed that "Charlie was boss" and that she had little recourse but to obey. For Marie Rose, who was raised in a strict Métis family, and who attended a convent where she received her education from Roman Catholic nuns, to witness this behaviour by her own husband and his friends was likely shocking and upsetting. This was particularly so as she was raising her own children in this environment. Writing about it may have been a way to process her shock of this behaviour.

26 Smith, *Eighty Years on the Plains*, 161–63.

1 Smith, *Eighty Years on the Plains*, 166.

2 MacKinnon, *The Identities of Marie Rose Delorme Smith*, 7.

3 Author unknown, as told by Marie Rose Delorme Smith, "Tribulations of Mrs. C. Smith of Pincher Creek, Alta., Smith," GAIA, Box 1, File 6, 1.

4 "Cayuse" refers, historically, to horses, typically the smaller and stockier horses that were thought to have been introduced in North America by the Spanish. These horses became a distinct breed and were named for the Cayuse People of eastern Washington and Oregon.

5 Jamaican ginger refers to Ginger Beer, which was a popular drink during the eighteenth century in Britain and North America.

6 The transcriber may have meant to convey that although Charlie had "rough ways" near the end of his life, he was thought of as having "good hearts." This is supported by Marie Rose's writing.

7 The term "fussing" is unclear. A possible explanation could be that he meant "missing."

8 The term "emcent" is unclear. The inference suggests that Marie Rose's horses may have been "neighing" and "scratching the ground" because they sensed that Charlie's horse (part of their own herd) was nearby. This would have been the expected horse behaviour of communication. Marie Rose reflects on this years later, noting that this intuitive call on the part of the horses was missed by the humans.

9 Smith, "Tribulations of Mrs. C. Smith of Pincher Creek, Alta., Smith," 1–8.

10 Shirley-Mae McCargar, interviews with the author, St. Albert, Alberta, October 2002 to July 2011.

11 Smith, *Eighty Years on the Plains*, 18–20.

12 Smith, *Eighty Years on the Plains*, 22.

13 Ibid.

14 Carter and McCormack, eds., "Lifelines," 18.

15 Marie Rose crossed out contents of this paragraph manually, with no indication of why. She may have been unsatisfied with how she had described her work and intended to re-type it in another location in her manuscript.

16 Smith, *Eighty Years on the Plains*, 21–23.

17 Kristen Burnett, *Taking Medicine: Women's Healing Work and Colonial Contact in Southern Alberta, 1880–1930* (UBC Press, 2010).

18 Smith, *Eighty Years on the Plains*, 73.

19 Smith, *Eighty Years on the Plains*, 73–77.

20 Smith, *Eighty Years on the Plains*, 81.

21 Smith, *Eighty Years on the Plains*, 81–84.

22 Lucy Eldersveld Murphy, "Women, Networks, and Colonization in Nineteenth Century Wisconsin," in *Contours of a People: Métis Family, Mobility, and History*, ed. St-Onge et. al. (University of Oklahoma Press, 2012), 245.

23 It is unclear who "Cooky" was. It is likely that it was a dog.

24 Smith, *Eighty Years on the Plains*, 166–67.

25 Smith, "The Adventures of the Wild West of 1870," 34.

26 Marie Rose does not use quotation marks, although the text suggests that she is quoting directly from words in the present. It appears that Marie Rose wrote from memory years after historical events. It is likely that her understanding of some events would have been

garnered through oral history shared with her by her network.

27 Marie Rose's reference to the "Blackfeet Treaty" is Treaty 7, signed in 1877 with the Siksika (Blackfoot), Kainai (Blood), Piikani (Peigan), Stoney Nakoda, and Tsuut'ina (Sarcee).

28 Marie Rose likely made this comment because the Métis were closely aligned with the Cree.

29 Smith, "The Adventures of the Wild West of 1870," 30–34.

30 Smith, "The Adventures of the Wild West," 35.

31 "Wavies" is a derivative of the Algonquian language and is "akin to the Ojibwa wêwe" goose.

32 Smith, "The Adventures of The Wild West of 1870," 35–36.

33 Farley Wuth "Lionel Brooke's Role as a Remittance Man," A Presentation to the Lethbridge Historical Society, October 19, 2004. See also: Farley Wuth, "A Colourful Character from Our Frontier Past: Remittance Man Lionel Brooke." Pincher Creek Historical Society, March 14, 2012.

34 Smith, "The Adventures of the Wild West," 37.

35 Marie Rose may have altered the spellings of specific Indigenous nations. The Stoney Nakoda "or îyârhe Nakodabi," are "culturally and linguistically allied to the Plains Assiniboine . . . they speak the northern dialect of the Dakota language." Their oral history confirms that their ancestors lived along the "Rocky Mountain foothills from time immemorial." Ian A. L. Getty, "Stoney-Nakoda," *The Canadian Encyclopedia*. Historica Canada. Article published February 7, 2006. Last edited May 24, 2021.

36 Marie Rose may have been referring to Whyte & Mackay Whisky, a brand that dates back to 1882.

37 It unclear who "Eastom" is in Marie Rose's writing. There remain families in the Pincher Creek area with the surname "Easton," so it is reasonable to assume the latter was the intended spelling.

38 Smith, "The Adventures of the Wild West," 37–38.

39 Smith, The Adventures of the Wild West of 1870," 63.

40 Ibid.

41 The Oldman River flows southeast to the Rocky Mountain foothills, along the Crowsnest and Castle Rivers. The Oldman River basin is in the traditional territory of the Piikani Nation of the Blackfoot Confederacy, and is named after "Napi, the Old Man," who, according to Indigenous Peoples, is "the creator of the Earth and all its living inhabitants."

42 Located in the Pincher Creek District, Mountain Mill was considered the "cradle of logging." In 1879, the Dominion government had established Mountain Mill as the first sawmill in the south-western Prairies and then was later sold to Senator Peter McLaren. Some of Marie Rose's family members lived in the Mountain Mill area. See Farley Wuth, "Frontier Chronicles of Mountain Mill," *Shootin' the Breeze* (April 17, 2017), https://archives.shootinthebreeze.ca/index.php/item/frontier-chronicles-of-mountain-mill.

43 Smith, The Adventures of the Wild West of 1870," 62–63.

44 Smith, "Adventures of the Wild West of 1870," 73.

45 Ibid.

46 Maria Campbell, "Foreword: Charting the Way," in *Contours of a People: Metis Family, Mobility, and History*, ed. St-Onge et. al. (University of Oklahoma Press, 2012), xiii.

47 Payment, *The Free People—Li Gens Libres*, 94–95.

48 Milch cows is in reference to cows kept for their milk.

49 Jock Carpenter, Marie Rose's granddaughter, notes in her book that "The Prairie Girl" was her own mother Mary Helene Smith Parfitt.

50 Today, "Walrond Ranche" is known as Waldron Ranch. It was established in 1883 at the time that Alberta's grasslands were being transformed into "cattle country." At that time, 260,000 acres of land was leased to Duncan McNab McEachran from Montreal, who established leases that stocked the ranch with 8,500 head of Hereford and Polled Angus cattle.

51 This is one of the few instances in which Marie Rose recorded her memories in French.

52 The correct name for "Rermaria" is Kermaria Convent. It has also been spelled "Ker Maria Convent."

53 In correspondence with Fr. Myles Gaffney, he confirms the names of the three sisters who came to Pincher Creek in 1904: Sister Mary Saint-Guenole, Sister Marie Saint-Alimene, and Sister Marie Angeligue du Sacre Couer, who was the first superior of the school. Email correspondence, April 24, 2024.

54 "Bishop Legal" was Émile-Joseph Legal, Oblate priest and then bishop who studied in France and was posted to the Canadian northwest where he ministered to Indigenous Peoples. He received the Blackfoot name Sspomitapi, meaning "he who sits on high."

55 Smith, "Adventures of the Wild West of 1870," 73–75.

1 Smith, "Does God Know His Business?" GAIA, File 6, 11.

2 Bailey Oster and Marilyn Lizee, eds., *Stories of Métis Women: Tales My Kookum Told Me* (Durvile & UpRoute Books, 2021), 64.

3 It is unclear if Marie Rose is referring to the area of British Columbia that is now designated a historic site, given that John George Brown came to be known as "Kootenai" Brown.

4 Marie Rose's use of the terms "half breeds" and "quarter breeds" demonstrates again that she subscribed to, at least in part, the racialized hierarchies of the day.

5 Kootenai Brown was buried on the shores of Waterton Lake. Next to him are the graves of his first wife Olive D'Loinais, sometimes spelled Olive Lyonnais, and his second wife, Cheepaythaquakasoon (Isabella) who he liked to refer to as Ni-chi-mous. Marie Rose spelled this name differently in various sections of her texts, including "Ni-ti-mous" and "Nichimous," though she most commonly used "Ni-chi-Mous." See: *Find a Grave*, https://www.findagrave.com/memorial/6290/john-george-brown; William Rodney, "BROWN, JOHN GEORGE, known as Kootenai Brown," in *Dictionary of Canadian Biography*, vol. 14, University of Toronto/Université Laval, 2003–, accessed April 11, 2025, https://www.biographi.ca/en/bio/brown_john_george_14E.html.

6 Smith, "Adventures of the Wild West of 1870," 40–42.

7 Jeanne Perreault, "'Memory Alive': An Inquiry into the Uses of Memory by Marilyn Dumont, Jeannette Armstronge, Louise Half, and Joy Harjo," in *Indigenous*

women and feminism: politics, activism, culture, ed. Cheryl Suzack et. al. (UBC Press, 2010), 201.

8 Payment, *The Free People—Li Gens Libres*, 141.

9 Smith, *Eighty Years on the Plains,* 59.

10 Payment, *The Free People—Li Gens Libres*, 42.

11 Payment, *The Free People—Li Gens Libres*, 147.

12 The use of the "Red Man" is another example of the use of an offensive term that Marie Rose used.

13 Smith, *Eighty Years on the Plains,* 56–59.

14 MacKinnon, *The Identities of Marie Rose Delorme Smith*, 48; William Rodney, *Kootenai Brown: The Unknown Frontiersman* (Heritage House Publishing, 1996), 10.

15 Smith, *Eighty Years on the Plains*, 125–26.

16 William Rodney, "BROWN, JOHN GEORGE, known as Kootenai Brown," in *Dictionary of Canadian Biography*, vol. 14, University of Toronto/Université Laval, 2003–, accessed April 11, 2025, https://www.biographi.ca/en/bio/brown_john_george_14E.html.

17 "Kootenai Brown's Grave," Galt Museum & Archives, accession no. 20151083180.

18 Smith, *Eighty Years on the Plains,* 124–27.

19 Smith, *Eighty Years on the Plains,* 131.

20 Margaret Osborne, "Early Women Were Hunters, Not Just Gatherers, Study Suggests," *Smithsonian Magazine* (June 30, 2023), https://www.smithsonianmag.com/smart-news/early-women-were-hunters-not-just-gatherers-study-suggests-180982459/.

21 Smith, *Eighty Years on the Plains,* 131–35.

22 Smith, "Does God Know His Business," 1–11.

23 Mrs. Hyrum Ririe, "Dear Mrs. Smith," November 21, 1941, GAIA, Box 1, File 2.

24 *Canadian Cattlemen: The Beef Magazine for Canadian Farmers*, https://www.canadiancattlemen.ca/.

25 Smith, "The Twenty Warnings," GAIA, File 5, 7–9.

26 Payment, *The Free People—Li Gens Libres*, 133. Payment notes that the Roman Catholic clergy agreed with the Métis regarding the "inaction and incompetence" of the territorial government. However, Father André was consulted by officials on how to encourage Riel to leave. Others, such as Marie Rose's uncle Norbert Delorme, were seen as "hotheads" who needed to be "controlled."

27 Smith, "The Twenty Warnings," 7–9.

28 Smith, "The Twenty Warnings,"48.

29 Claim jumpers were those who staked a claim on land previously occupied or claimed, in this case by the Métis people as new settlers arrived.

30 Smith, "The Twenty Warnings," 48.

31 Ibid.

CHAPTER 5: MATRIARCH

1 Smith, "The Twenty Warnings," 48.

2 Smith, *Eighty Years on the Plains,* 174.

3 Eliane Leslau Silverman, *The Last Best West: Women on the Alberta Frontier, 1880–1930* (Eden Press, 1984).

4 Nathalie Kermoal, "Métis Women's Environmental Knowledge and the Recognition of Métis Rights," in *Living on the Land: Indigenous Women's Understanding of Place*, ed. Nathalie Kermoal and Isabel Altamirano-Jiménez (AU Press, 2016), 109.

5 Smith, "The Adventures of the Wild West of 1870," 13.

6 Ibid.

7 Smith, "The Adventures of the Wild West of 1870," 13–16.

8 Smith, "The Adventures of the Wild West of 1870," 29.

9 These customs were most likely Plains Cree. Referring to them as a "queer people" strongly suggests that Marie Rose was writing for a settler audience. In fact, the Métis were close allies of the Cree, and shared many of the same customs.

10 The Sun Dance is an annual First Nations sacred ceremony that was performed on the Prairies. It was forbidden by the Indian Act in 1895, and given Marie Rose's own positionality, it is perhaps understandable that she would deem these ceremonies, at least in her writing, a problem. The fact that she provided such detail speaks not only to her in depth and first-hand knowledge, but also to her acceptance of these important cultural practices.

11 Smith, "The Adventures of the Wild West of 1870," 26–29.

12 Smith, "The Adventures of the Wild West of 1870," 48.

13 Murphy, "Women, Networks, and Colonization in Nineteenth-Century Wisconsin," 245.

14 Diane P. Payment, "Une Femme En Vaut Deux—'Strong Like Two People,' Marie Fisher Gaudet of Fort Good Hope, Northwest Territories," in *Contours of a People: Metis Family, Mobility, and History*, ed. St-Onge et. al. (University of Oklahoma Press, 2012), 265.

15 Smith, "The Adventures of the Wild West of 1870," 49.

16 Smith, "The Adventures of the Wild West of 1870," 48–49.

17 Burnett, *Taking Medicine*, 42.

18 Burnett, *Taking Medicine*, 4.

19 Kermoal, "Métis Women's Environmental Knowledge and the Recognition of Métis Rights," 123.

20 Carpenter, *Fifty Dollar Bride*, 39.

21 Smith, "The Adventures of the Wild West of 1870," 46; Edith Fowke, ed., *The Penguin Book of Canadian Folk Songs*, (Penguin Books Canada, 1986). Fowke suggests on page 204 that the folk song was sung in at least five Canadian provinces before 1896.

22 Kermoal, "Métis Women's Environmental Knowledge and the Recognition of Métis Rights," 132.

23 It was more common for the Métis to play the fiddle. Marie Rose's reference to the violin reflected the influence of the Roman Catholic nuns in the convent. This influence extended beyond her choice of musical instruments but also to her choice of descriptors for Indigenous Peoples and their customs.

24 Smith, "The Adventures of the Wild West of 1870," 46–47.

25 Smith, *Eighty Years on the Plains,* 174.

26 Foggo, "Assembling Auntie."

27 Smith, *Eighty Years on the Plains,* 173–74.

28 Sarah Carter, *Imperial Plots: Women, Land, and the Spadework of British Colonialism on the Canadian Prairies* (University of Manitoba Press, 2016).

29 Jacinthe Duval, "The Catholic Church and the Formation of Métis identity," *Past Imperfect* 9 (2001), 66.

30 Smith, Untitled note, GAIA, 85–86.

CHAPTER 6: WIDOWED HOMESTEADER

1 Smith, "The Adventures of the Wild West of 1870," no page number.

2 Carter, *Imperial Plots*, 49.

3 Carter, *Imperial Plots*, 164–65.

4 Smith, "Instant death in a most horrible manner," GAIA, File 6, no page number.

5 Bill Ganzel, Living History Farm, "Riding the Rails," 2003, accessed May 18, 2023, https://livinghistoryfarm.org/farming-in-the-1930s/water/riding-the-rails/. Also see, Encyclopedia.com, "Riding the Rails 1929–1941," accessed May 18, 2023, https://www.encyclopedia.com/education/news-and-education-magazines/riding-rails-1929-1941.

6 Chris Zdeb, "Oct. 1, 1932: No more free rides for hoboes," *Edmonton Journal* (October 1, 2014), accessed May 18 2023, https://edmontonjournal.com/news/local-news/oct-1-1932-no-more-free-rides-for-hoboes.

7 Smith, *Eighty Years on the Plains,* 89.

8 Smith, *Eighty Years on the Plains,* 86–89.

9 While a family member provided a handwritten annotation about Marie Rose's death, it has been confirmed that she was ninety-nine years old when she passed away. Smith, "The Adventures of the Wild West of 1870," no page number.

10 Smith, "Instant death in a Most Horrible manner."

CHAPTER 7: PIONEER OF THE PLAINS

1 Pincher Creek Historical Society, *Prairie Grass to Mountain Pass: History of the Pioneers of Pincher Creek and District* (Pincher Creek Historical Society, 1974), 249.

2 Carpenter, *Fifty Dollar Bride*, 149.

3 Burnet, *Taking Medicine*, 55–56; Frog Lake Community Club, *Land of Red and White* (Frog Lake Community Club, 1977), 98.

4 Burnett, *Taking Medicine*, 59.

5 Burnett, *Taking Medicine*, 60.

6 Parks Canada, "Marie Rose (Delorme) Smith National Historic Person (1861–1960)," accessed June 2, 2025, https://parks.canada.ca/culture/designation/personnage-person/marie-rose-delorme.

7 "South Alberta Pioneer Passes in Lethbridge," *Pincher Creek Echo* 60, no. 34 (April 7, 1960), 1.

8 "Married Noted Furtrader: Life on the Plains in Frontier Days Recalled by Pioneer Lady," *Lethbridge Herald* (September 24, 1954), 6.

9 Emma Lynch-Staunton, "Eighty Years on the Plains: The Story of Mrs. Charles Smith, Pincher Creek," *The Lethbridge Herald* (November 14, 1941), 16.

10 Pincher Creek Echo, "Pincher Creek Hard Hit By the War This Week: Two Well-Known Families Bereaved," *Pincher Creek Echo* (September 7, 1917), 1.

Bibliography

INTERVIEWS

McCargar, Shirley-Mae. Interviews with the author, St. Alberta, AB, October 2005-July 2011.

Smith, Marie Rose Delorme. "Tribulations of Mrs. C. Smith of Pincher Creek Alta by Mrs. C. Smith." Transcribed by Ben Montgomery, late 1930s. GAIA, Accession No. 998.121.19, File 6.

ARCHIVES

Glenbow-Alberta Institute Archives

Galt Museum & Archives

PUBLISHED PRIMARY SOURCES

Lynch-Staunton, Emma. "Eighty Years on the Plains: The Story of Mrs. Charles Smith, Pincher Creek." *The Lethbridge Herald*, November 14, 1941.

"Married Noted Furtrader: Life on the Plains in Frontier Days Recalled by Pioneer Lady." *The Lethbridge Herald*, September 24, 1954.

"Pincher Creek Hard Hit By the War This Week: Two Well-Known Families Bereaved." *Pincher Creek Echo*, September 7, 1917.

Zdeb, Chris. "Oct. 1, 1932: No more free rides for hoboes," *Edmonton Journal* (October 1, 2014).

PUBLISHED SECONDARY SOURCES

Burnett, Kristin. *Taking Medicine: Women's Healing Work and Colonial Contact in Southern Alberta, 1880–1930*. UBC Press, 2011.

Campbell, Maria. "Foreword: Charting the Way." In *Contours of a People: Metis Family, Mobility, and History*, edited by Nicole St-Onge, Carolyn Podruchny, and Brenda Macdougall. University of Oklahoma Press, 2012.

Carpenter, Jock. *Fifty Dollar Bride: Marie Rose Smith—A Chronicle of Métis Life in the 19th Century*. Gray's Publishing, 1977.

Carter, Sarah. *Imperial Plots: Women, Land, and the Spadework of British Colonialism on the Canadian Prairies*. University of Manitoba Press, 2016.

———. "The Montana Memories of Emma Minesinger: Windows on the Family Work, and Boundary Culture of a Borderlands Woman." In *Recollecting: Lives of Aboriginal Women of the Canadian Northwest and Borderlands*, edited by Sarah Carter and Patricia A. McCormack. AU Press, 2011.

Carter, Sarah, and Patricia A. McCormack, eds. *Recollecting: Lives of Aboriginal Women of the Canadian Northwest and Borderlands*. AU Press, 2011.

Duval, Jacinthe. "The Catholic Church and the Formation of Metis identity." *Past Imperfect* 9, 2001 2003.

Eldersveld Murphy, Lucy. "Women, Networks, and Colonization in Nineteenth Century Wisconsin." In *Contours of a People: Metis Family, Mobility, and History*, edited by Nicole St-Onge, Carolyn Podruchny, and Brenda Macdougall. University of Oklahoma Press, 2012.

Fowke, Edith, ed. *The Penguin Book of Canadian Folk Songs*. Penguin Books Canada, 1986.

Kermoal, Nathalie. "Métis Women's Environmental Knowledge and the Recognition of Métis Rights," in *Living on the Land: Indigenous Women's Understanding of Place*, edited by Nathalie Kermoal and Isabel Altamirano-Jimenez. AU Press, 2016.

Macdougall, Brenda, Carolyn Podruchny, and Nicole St-Onge. "Introduction: Cultural Mobility and the Contours of Difference." In *Contours of a People: Metis Family, Mobility, and History*. Edited by Nicole St-Onge, Carolyn Podruchny, and Brenda Macdougall. University of Oklahoma Press, 2012.

Macdougall, Brenda. *Contours of a People: Métis Family, Mobility, and History*. University of Oklahoma Press, 2012.

MacKinnon, Doris Jeanne. *Metis Pioneers: Marie Rose Delorme Smith and Isabella Clark Hardisty Lougheed*. University of Alberta Press, 2018.

———. *The Identities of Marie Rose Delorme Smith: Portrait of a Métis Woman, 1861–1960*. University of Regina Press, 2012.

Oster, Bailey, and Marilin Lizee, eds. *Stories of Métis Women: Tales My Kookum Told Me*. Durville Publications, 2021.

Payment, Diane. *The Free People—Li Gens Libres: A History of the Métis Community of Batoche, Saskatchewan*. University of Calgary Press, 2009.

———. "Une Femme En Vaut Deux—'Strong Like Two People': Marie Fisher Gaudet of Fort Good Hope, Northwest Territories." In *Contours of a People:*

Metis Family, Mobility, and History. Edited by Nicole St-Onge, Carolyn Podruchny, and Brenda Macdougall. University of Oklahoma Press, 2012.

Perreault, Jeanne. "'Memory Alive': An Inquiry into the Uses of Memory by Marilyn Dumont, Jeannette Armstronge, Louise Half, and Joy Harjo." In *Indigenous women and feminism: politics, activism, culture*, edited by Cheryl Suzack, Shari M. Huhndorf, Jeanne Perreault, and Jean Barman. UBC Press, 2010.

Rupertsland Institute, Métis in Alberta: Métis Foundational Knowledge Theme. Rupertsland Institute, 2022.

Sleeper-Smith, Susan. *Indian Women and French Men: Rethinking Cultural Encounter in the Western Great Lakes*. University of Massachusetts Press, 2006.

Wonders, William C. "Far Corner of the Strange Empire Central Alberta on the Eve of Homestead Settlement." *Great Plains Quarterly* 3, no. 2 (Spring 1983).

POPULAR SOURCES

Canadian Cattleman: The Beef Magazine for Canadian Farmers.

Foggo, Cheryl. "Assembling Auntie: Illuminating a long-forgotten pioneer." *albertaviews: The Magazine for Engaged Citizens*, January 1, 2009.

Frog Lake Community Club. *Land of Red and White*. Frog Lake Community Club, 1977.

Pincher Creek Historical Society. *Prairie Grass to Mountain Pass: History of the Pioneers of Pincher Creek and District*. Pincher Creek Historical Society, 1974.

Rodney, William. *Kootenai Brown: The Unknown Frontiersman*. Heritage House Publishing, 1996.

Silverman, Elaine Leslau. *The Last Best West: Women on the Alberta Frontier, 1880–1930*. Eden Press, 1984.

Wuth, Farley. "A Colourful Character from Our Frontier Past: Remittance Man Lionel Brooke." Pincher Creek Historical Society. 14 March 2012. "Lionel Brooke's Role as a Remittance Man." A Presentation to the Lethbridge Historical Society, 19 October 2004.

ONLINE SOURCES

Blackfoot Crossing Historical Park. Blackfootcrossing.ca. "About." Accessed October 2, 2023. https://blackfoot-crossing.ca/wordpress/about/.

Hodgson-Bright, Kris. "Battle of the Belly River." YouTube, 2024. https://www.youtube.com/watch?v=3auWH4uxjGA.

Canadian Geographic. "Métis: Material Culture." Indigenous Peoples Atlas of Canada. Undated. Accessed on October 15, 2023. https://indigenouspeoplesatlasof-canada.ca/article/material-culture/.

Conn, Heather. "Cuthbert Grant." *The Canadian Encyclopedia*. Historica Canada. Article published January 30, 2018. Last edited January 25, 2023. https://www.thecanadianencyclopedia.ca/en/article/cuthbert-grant.

Elias, Peter Douglas. "Dakota." *The Canadian Encyclopedia*. Historica Canada. Article published December 12, 2010. Last Edited March 2, 2017. https://www.thecanadi-anencyclopedia.ca/en/article/dakota.

Encyclopedia.com. "Riding the Rails 1929–1941." Accessed May 18, 2023. https://www.encyclopedia.

com/education/news-and-education-magazines/riding-rails-1929-1941.

Filice, Michelle. "Dene Games." *The Canadian Encyclopedia*. Historica Canada. Article published December 5, 2016. Last Edited November 10, 2023. https://www.thecanadianencyclopedia.ca/en/article/dene-games.

Find a Grave. https://www.findagrave.com/memorial/6290/john-george-brown.

"Fort Garry—Fort Edmonton trail National Historic Event." Directory of Federal Heritage Designations, 1989. Accessed on September 29, 2023. https://www.pc.gc.ca/apps/dfhd/page_nhs_eng.aspx?id=1588.

Foster, John E. "Pemmican Proclamation." *The Canadian Encyclopedia*. Article published February 7, 2006. https://www.thecanadianencyclopedia.ca/en/article/pemmican-proclamation.

Ganzel, Bill. Living History Farm, "Riding the Rails," 2003. Accessed May 18, 2023. https://livinghistoryfarm.org/farming-in-the-1930s/water/riding-the-rails/.

Getty, Ian A.L. "Stoney-Nakoda." *The Canadian Encyclopedia*. Historica Canada. Article published February 7, 2006. Last edited May 24, 2021. https://www.thecanadianencyclopedia.ca/en/article/stoney-nakoda.

Government of Canada. "The Numbered Treaties." Accessed on October 3, 2023. https://www.rcaanc-cirnac.gc.ca/eng/1360948213124/1544620003549.

Jamas-Abra, Erin. "Greater Prairie Chicken." *The Canadian Encyclopedia*. Historica Canada. Article published January 25, 2023. https://www.thecanadianencyclopedia.ca/en/article/greater-prairie-chicken.

Livesay, Nora and John D. Nichols, eds. The Ojibwe People's Dictionary. Accessed April 11, 2025. https://ojibwe.lib.umn.edu/main-entry/makoons-na.

Manitoba Métis Federation. "Pemmican." Accessed May 1, 2023. https://www.mmf.mb.ca/Métisminute/pemmican.

McNab, Miriam. "Indigenous Women's Issues in Canada." *The Canadian Encyclopedia*. Historica Canada. Article published February 7, 2006; Last Edited April 30, 2020. https://www.thecanadianencyclopedia.ca/en/article/native-womens-issues.

Osborne, Margaret. "Early Women Were Hunters, Not Just Gatherers, Study Suggests." *Smithsonian Magazine*, June 30, 2023. Accessed September 23, 2023. https://www.smithsonianmag.com/smart-news/early-women-were-hunters-not-just-gatherers-study-suggests-180982459/.

Parks Canada. "Marie Rose (Delorme) Smith National Historic Person (1861-1960). Accessed October 15, 2023. https://parks.canada.ca/culture/designation/personnage-person/marie-rose-delorme.

Rodney, William. "Brown, John George, Kootenai Brown." *Dictionary of Canadian Biography* Vol. 14, University of Toronto/Université Laval, 2003. Accessed on September 21, 2023. http://www.biographi.ca/en/bio/brown_john_george_14E.html.

Rural Municipality of St. François Xavier. "A Brief History of the RM of St. François Xavier." Accessed April 11, 2025. https://www.rm-stfrancois.mb.ca/p/history.

Tesar, Alex. "Treaty 7." *The Canadian Encyclopedia*. Historica Canada. Article published August 19, 2016. Last Edited November 10, 2023. https://www.thecanadianencyclopedia.ca/en/article/treaty-7.

Wuth, Farley. "Frontier Chronicles of Mountain Mill." *Shootin' the Breeze*. April 17, 2017. https://archives.shootinthebreeze.ca/index.php/item/frontier-chronicles-of-mountain-mill.

Index

n denotes references to endnotes.

More from Doris Jeanne MacKinnon…

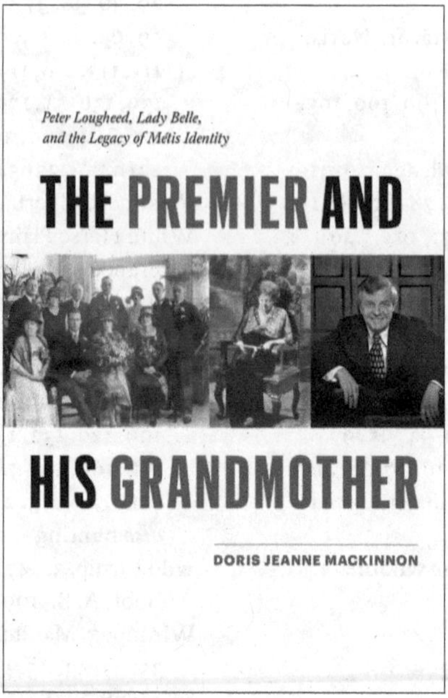

THE PREMIER AND HIS GRANDMOTHER

Peter Lougheed, Lady Belle, and the Legacy of Métis Identity

COMBINING POLITICAL BIOGRAPHY AND HISTORICAL NARRATIVE, *The Premier and His Grandmother* introduces readers to two compelling and complex public figures in Alberta history.

Born into a prominent fur trading family and known in elite circles as Lady Belle, Isabella Clark Hardisty Lougheed (1861–1936) established a distinct role for herself as an influential Métis woman in southern Alberta at a time when racial boundaries in the province were hardening and Métis activists had laid a firm foundation for their community to be recognized as distinct Indigenous Peoples.

Isabella's grandson Edgar Peter Lougheed (1928–2021) served as premier of Alberta at a time that saw success and hardship in the realm of Indigenous activism. Drawing on Peter Lougheed's personal papers, family interviews, and archival research, this book analyzes his political initiatives in the context of his own identity as a person of Métis ancestry. While there are several publications that refer to Peter Lougheed in the context of his role as premier, few have acknowledged his connection to an important Métis pioneer family and his Indigenous ancestors. This intriguing book draws parallels between grandmother and grandson, exploring how Métis identity, political activism, and colonial institutional power shaped the lives and legacies of both.

DORIS JEANNE MACKINNON was born on a farm in northeastern Alberta and attended school in the historic town of St-Paul-des-Métis. She holds a PhD in Indigenous and post-Confederation Canadian history. An independent researcher, author, and post-secondary instructor, she lives in Central Alberta and on Vancouver Island. Her publications, including the bestselling *The Premier and His Grandmother* and *Métis Matriarchs: Agents of Transition* (co-edited with Cheryl Troupe), focus on Métis women and Western Canadian topics that expand readers' understanding of our diverse people and experiences. Her books are written in an engaging style that appeals to a broad cross-section of the population.

MARIE ROSE DELORME SMITH (1861–1960) was a Métis woman born during the fur trade era. Married at sixteen to a robe-and-whiskey trader several years her senior, Marie Rose spent most of her adult life in Pincher Creek, Alberta, where she became a homesteader, raised seventeen children, established a boarding house, served as a medicine woman and midwife, and published numerous articles in the periodical,

Canadian Cattlemen. Her writing, both published and unpublished, sheds light on Métis identity during a period of cultural, political, and economic change. In 2022, she was designated a person of national historic significance by the Government of Canada.

DONALD McCARGAR is a member of the Métis Nation of Alberta and is the great-grandson of Marie Rose Delorme Smith.